Lovely Pug
Dog Coloring Book

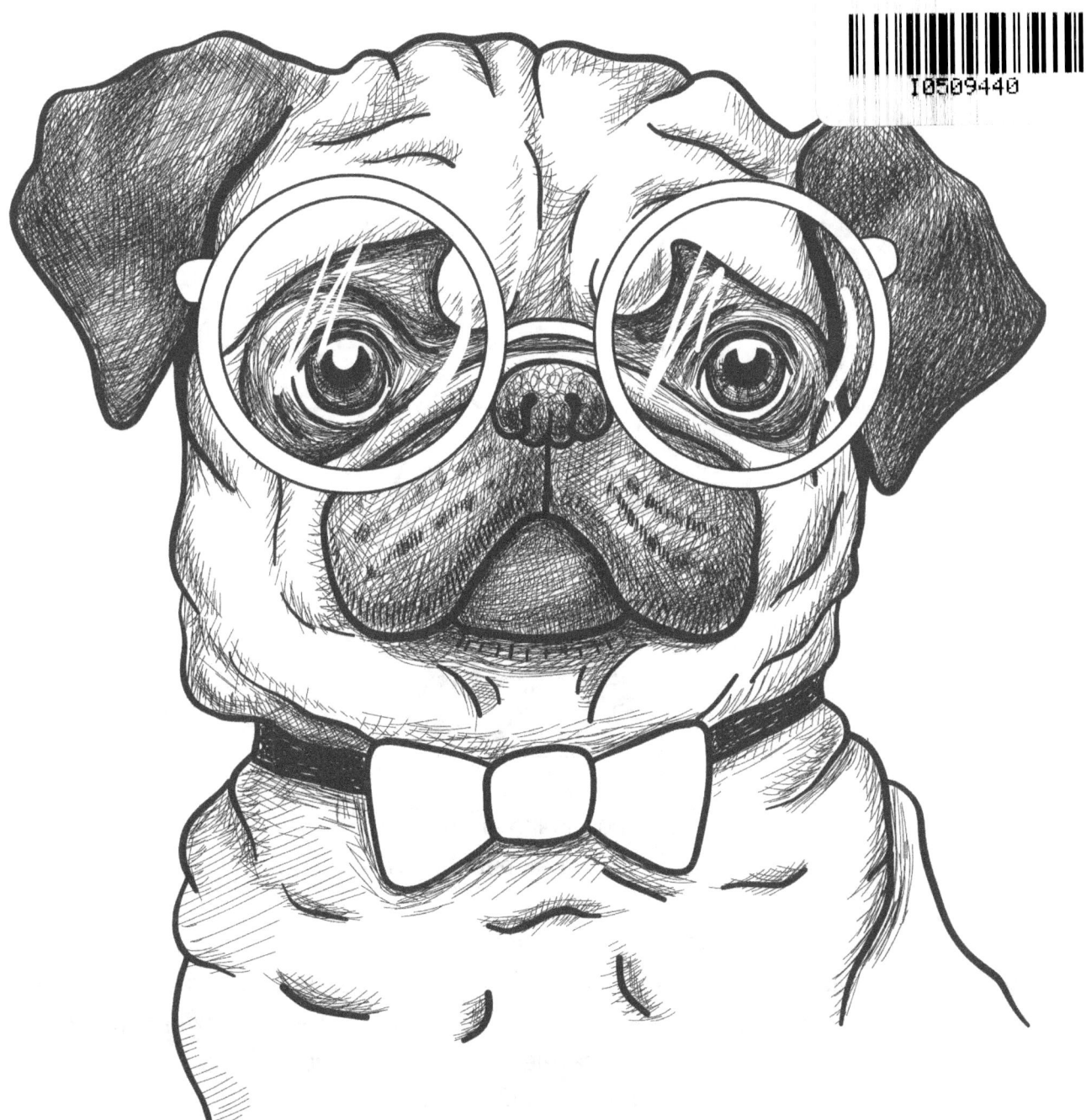

An Adults Coloring Book

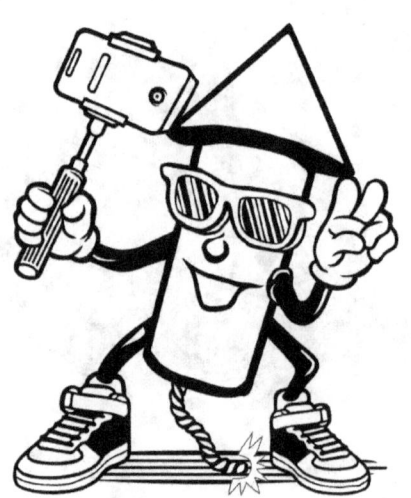

PUBLISHED IN 2020 BY
FIREWORK PUBLISHING

COPYRIGHT 'ILLUSTRATIONS' 2020 FIREWORK PUBLISHING
ALL RIGHT RESERVED.'NO PART OF THIS PUBLICATION MAY BE REPRODUCED OR TRANSMITTED IN ANY FORM OR BY ANY MEANS, ELECTRONIC OR MECHANICAL, INCLUDING PHOTOCOPY RECORDING OR ANY INFORMATION STORAGE SYSTEM AND RETRIEVAL SYSTEM WITHOUT PERMISSION IN WRITING
BY FIREWORK PUBLISHING

PRINTED IN THE UNITED STATE OF AMERICA

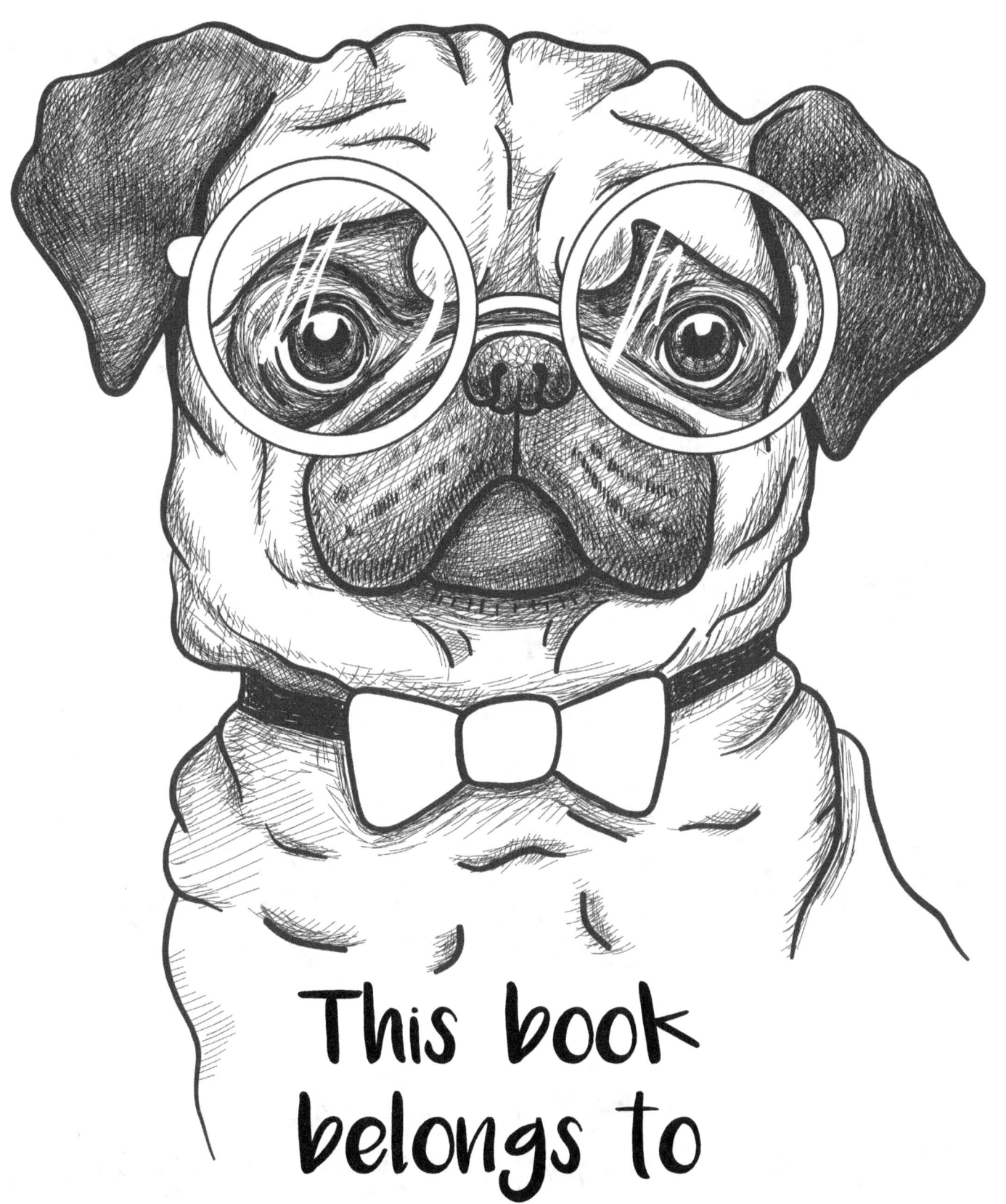

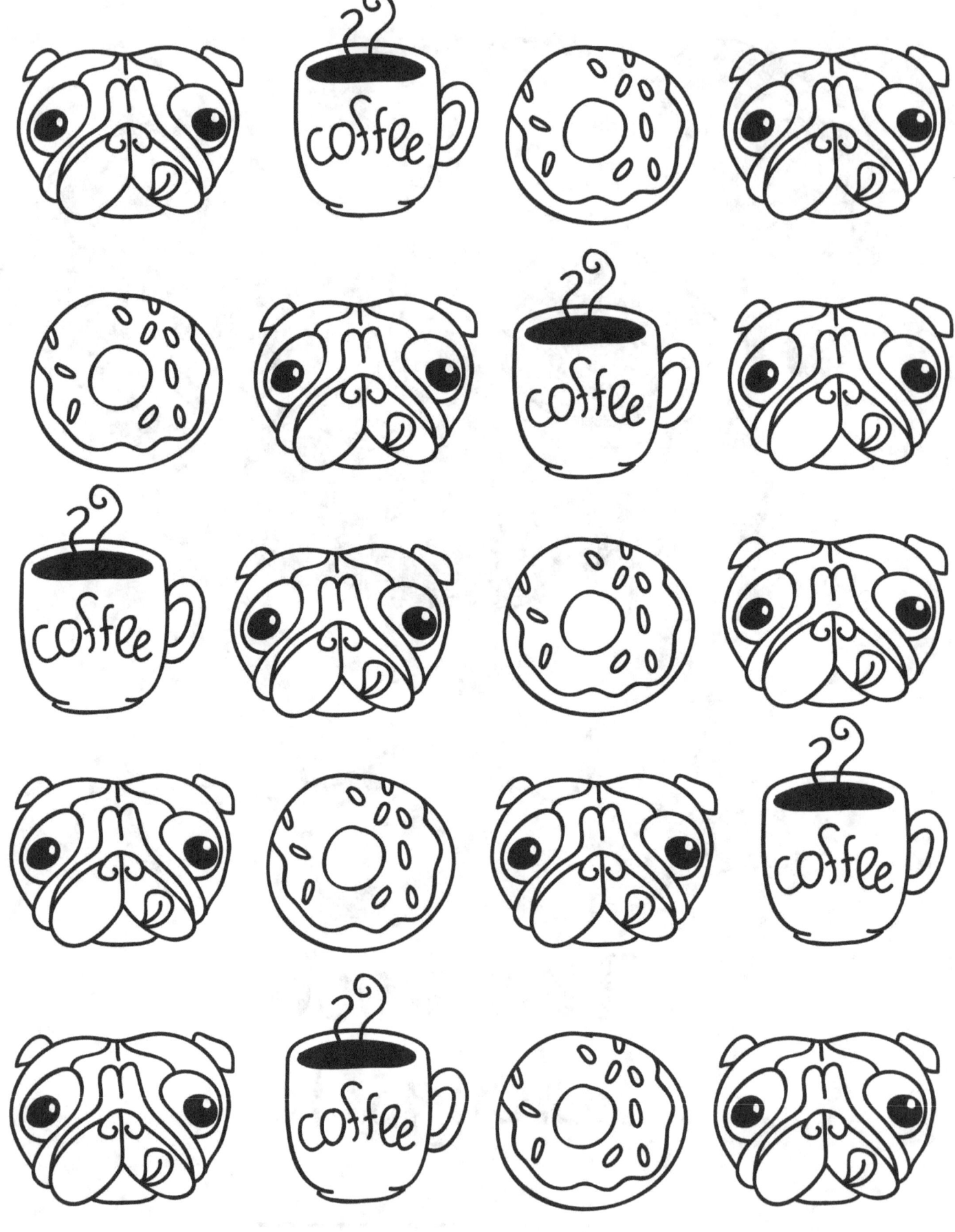

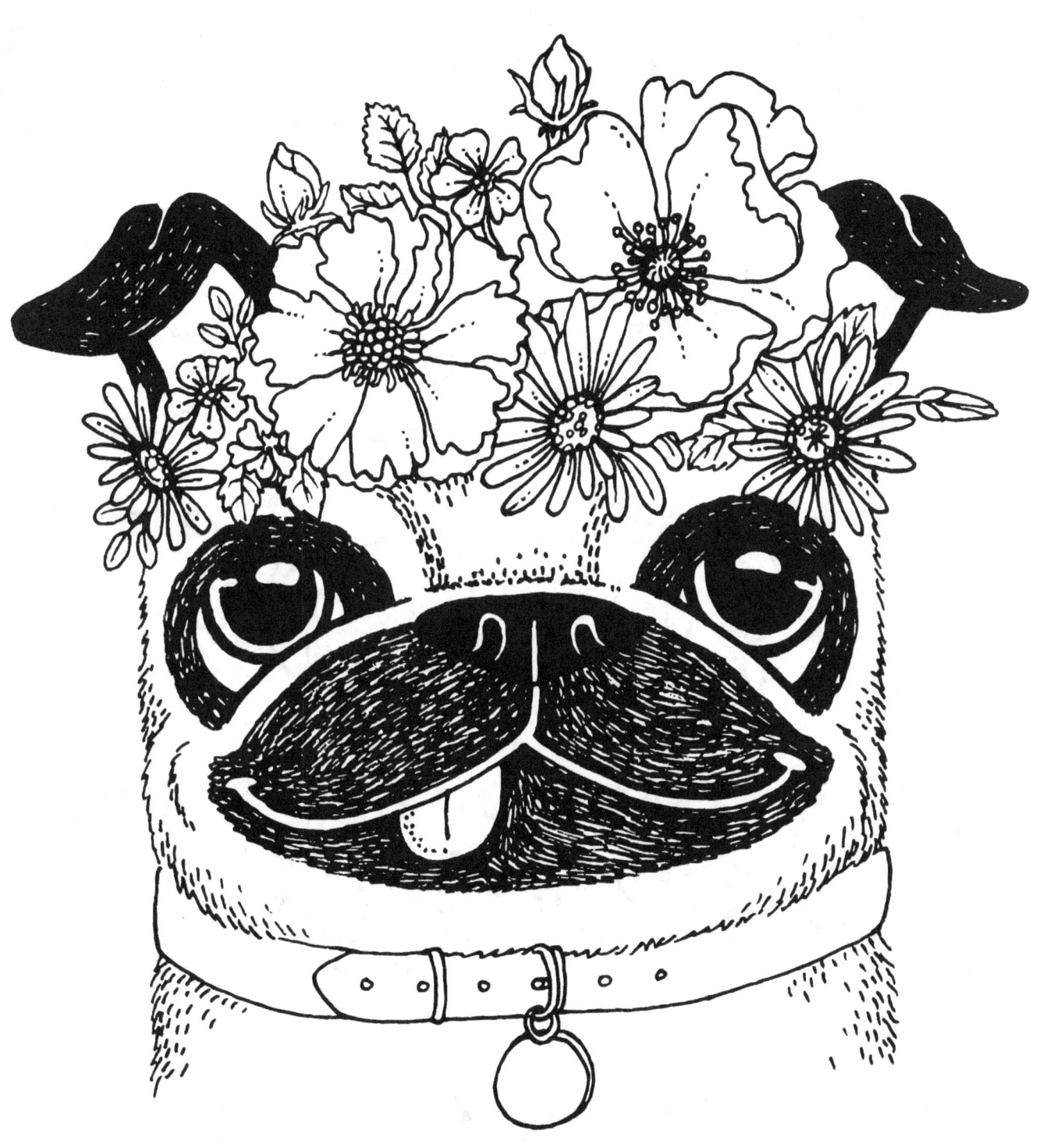

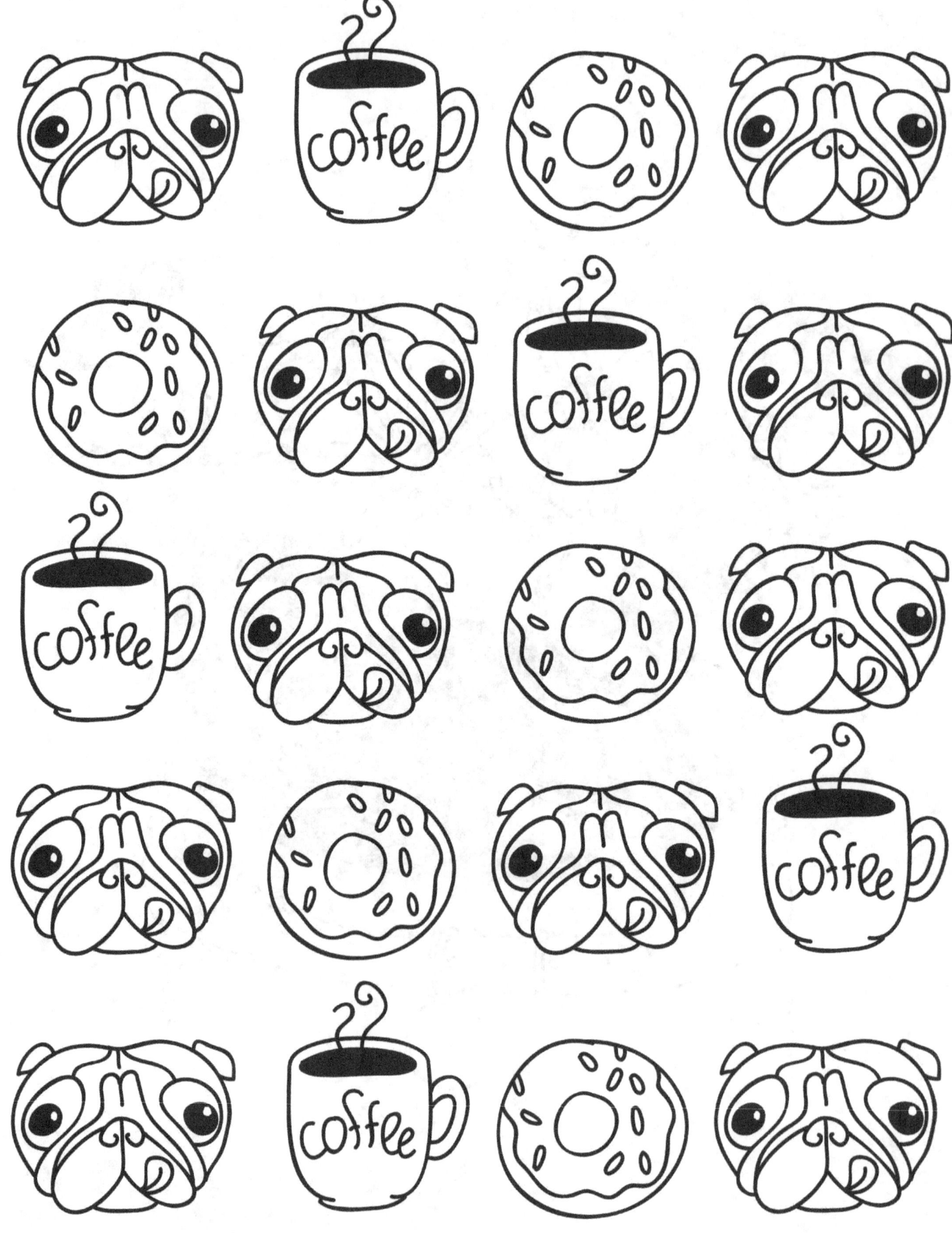

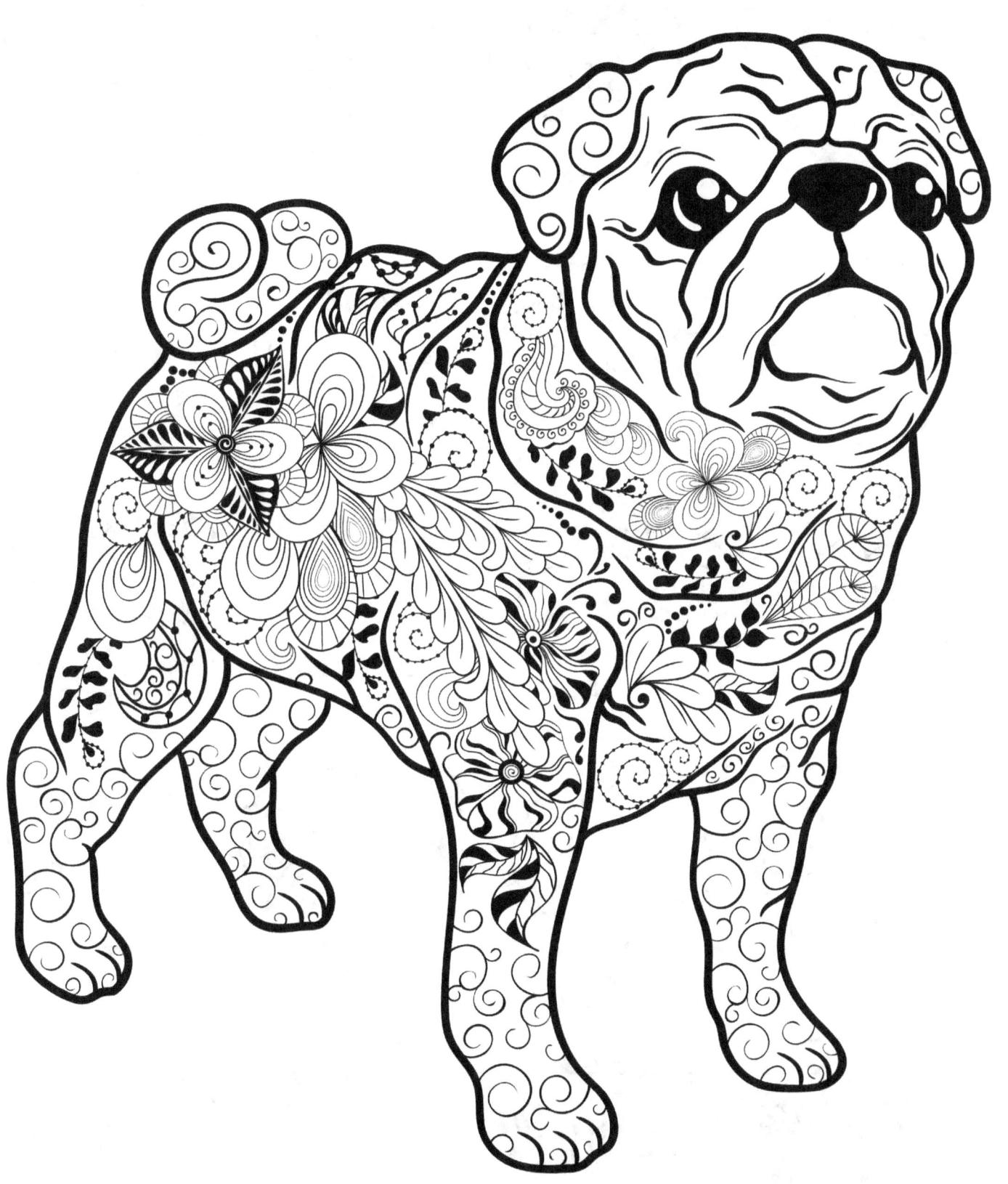

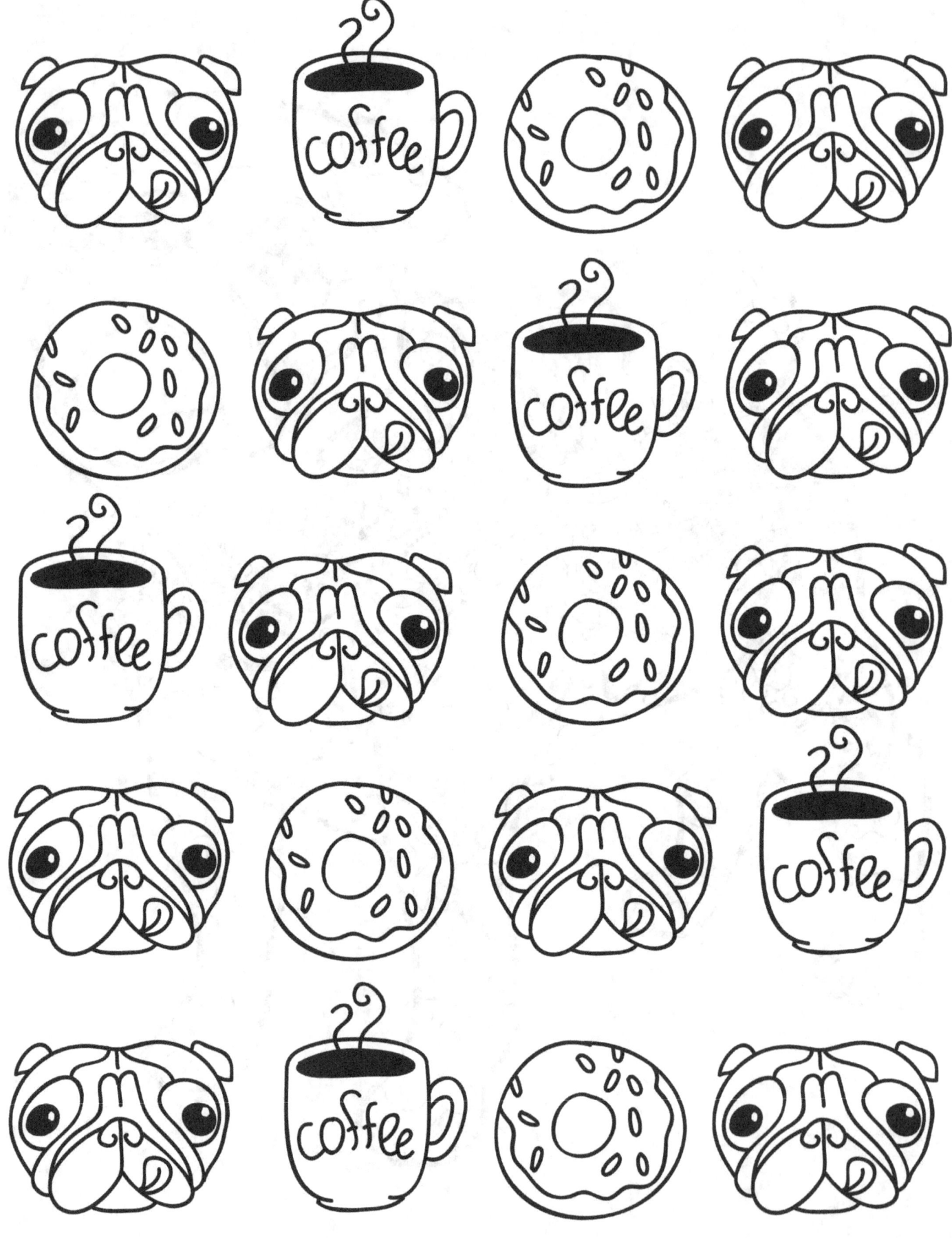

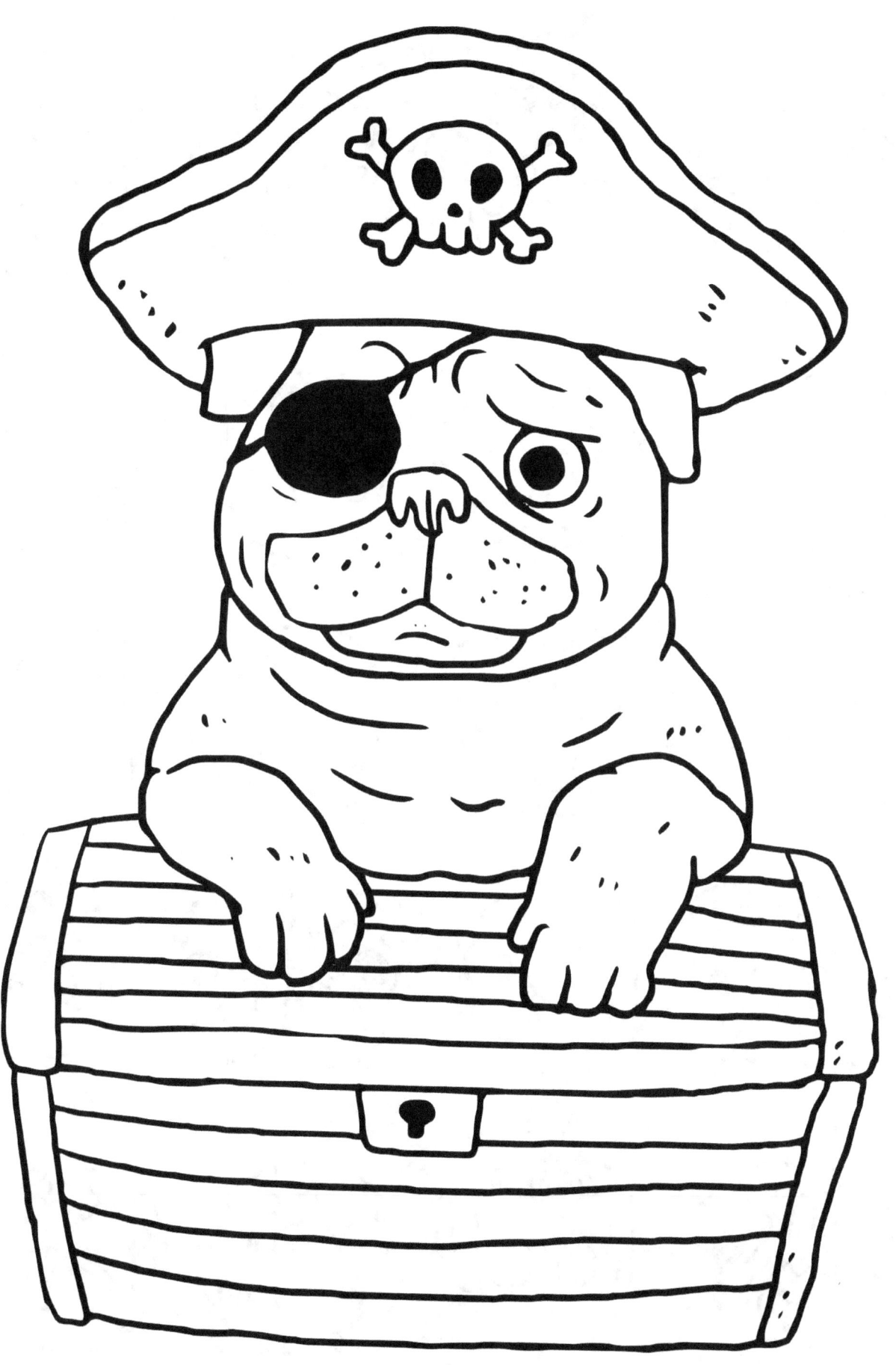

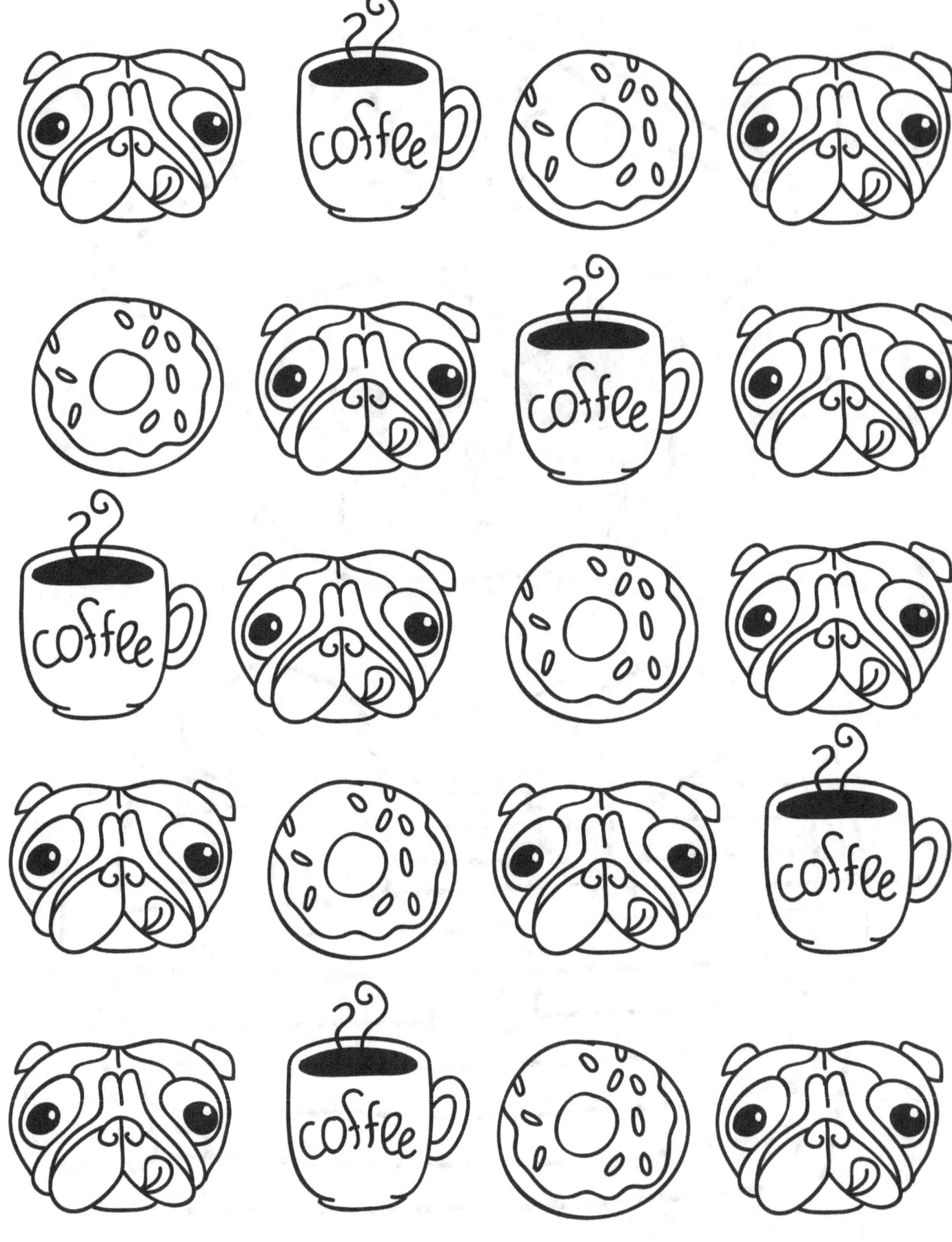

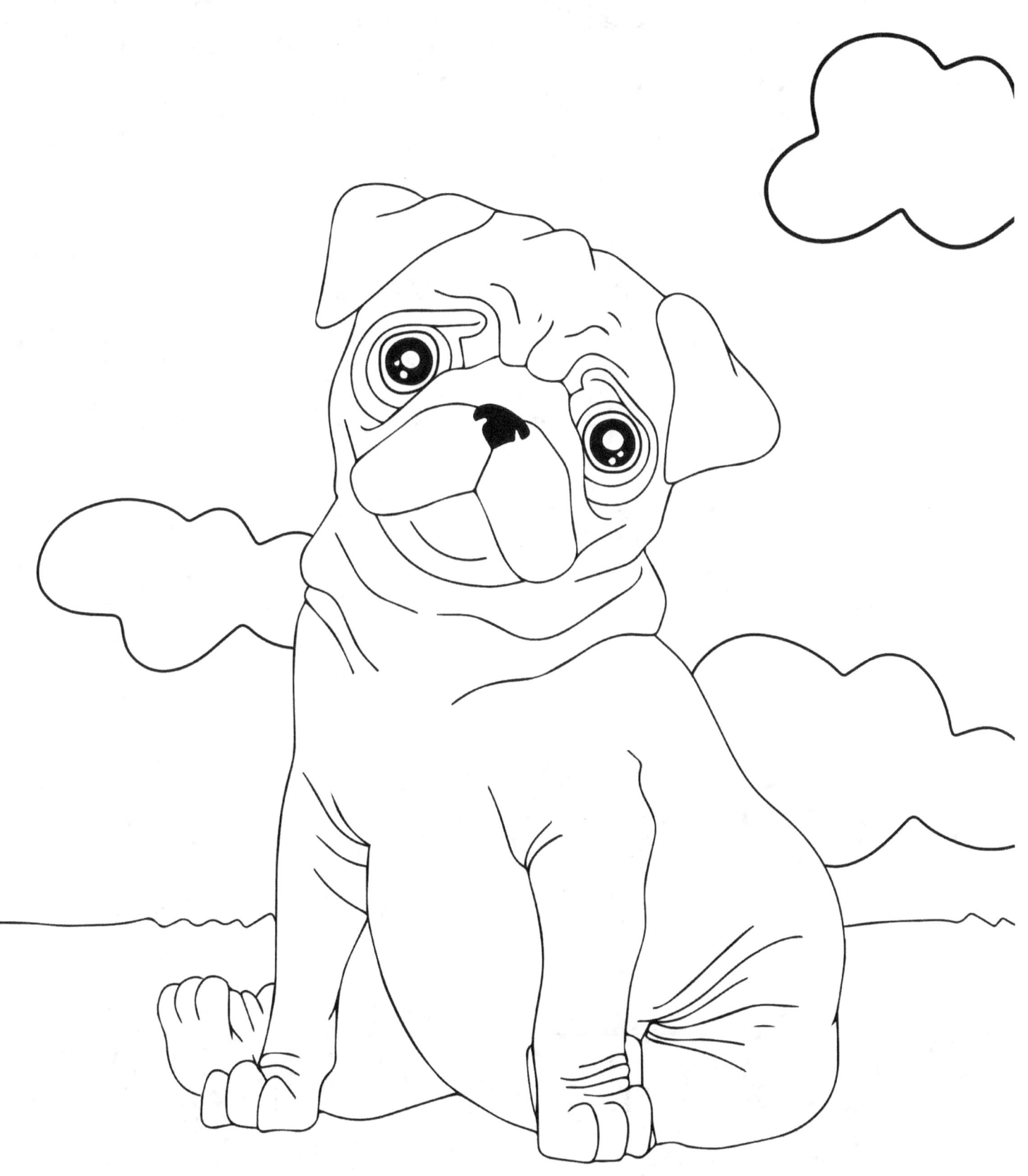

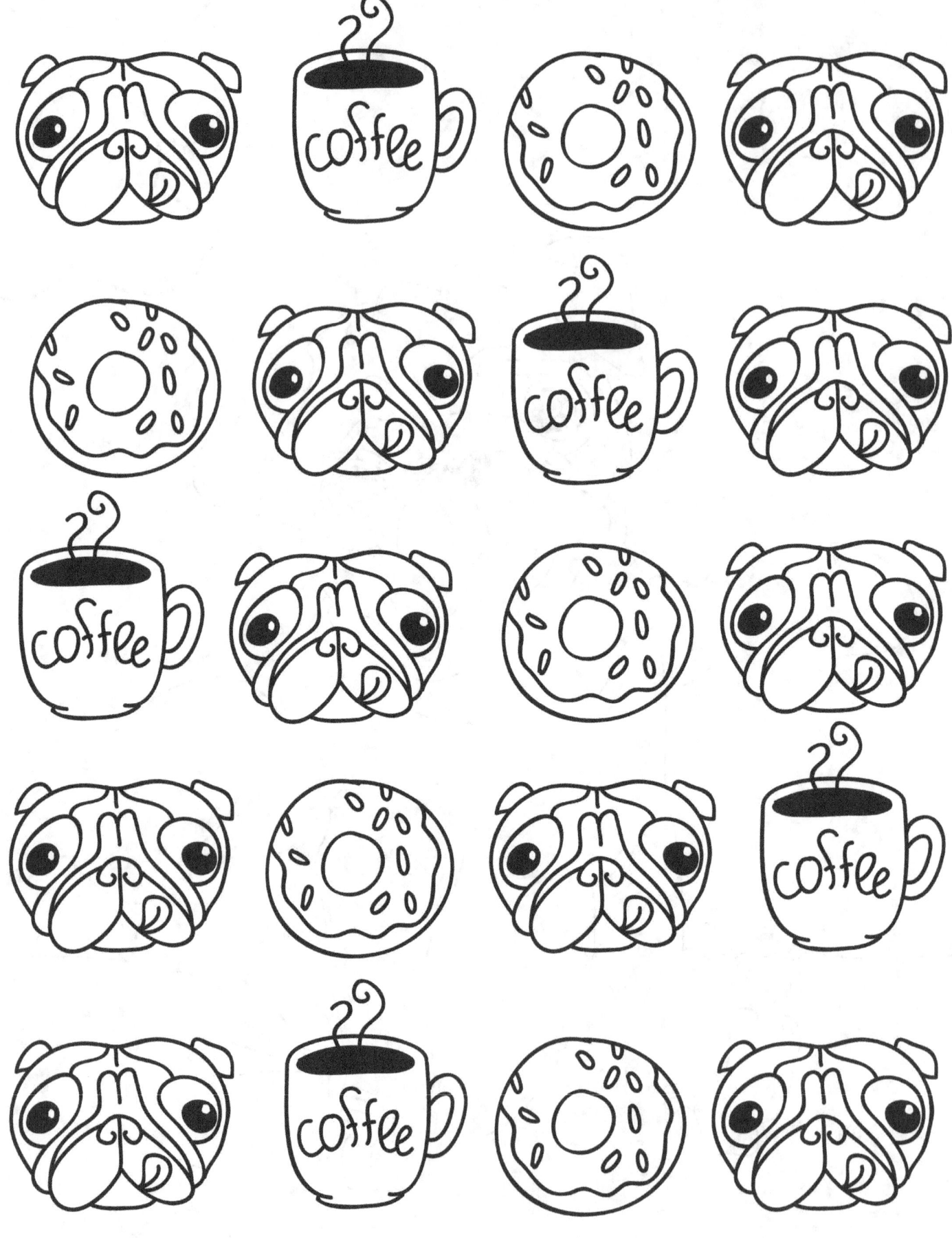

I'm unicorn

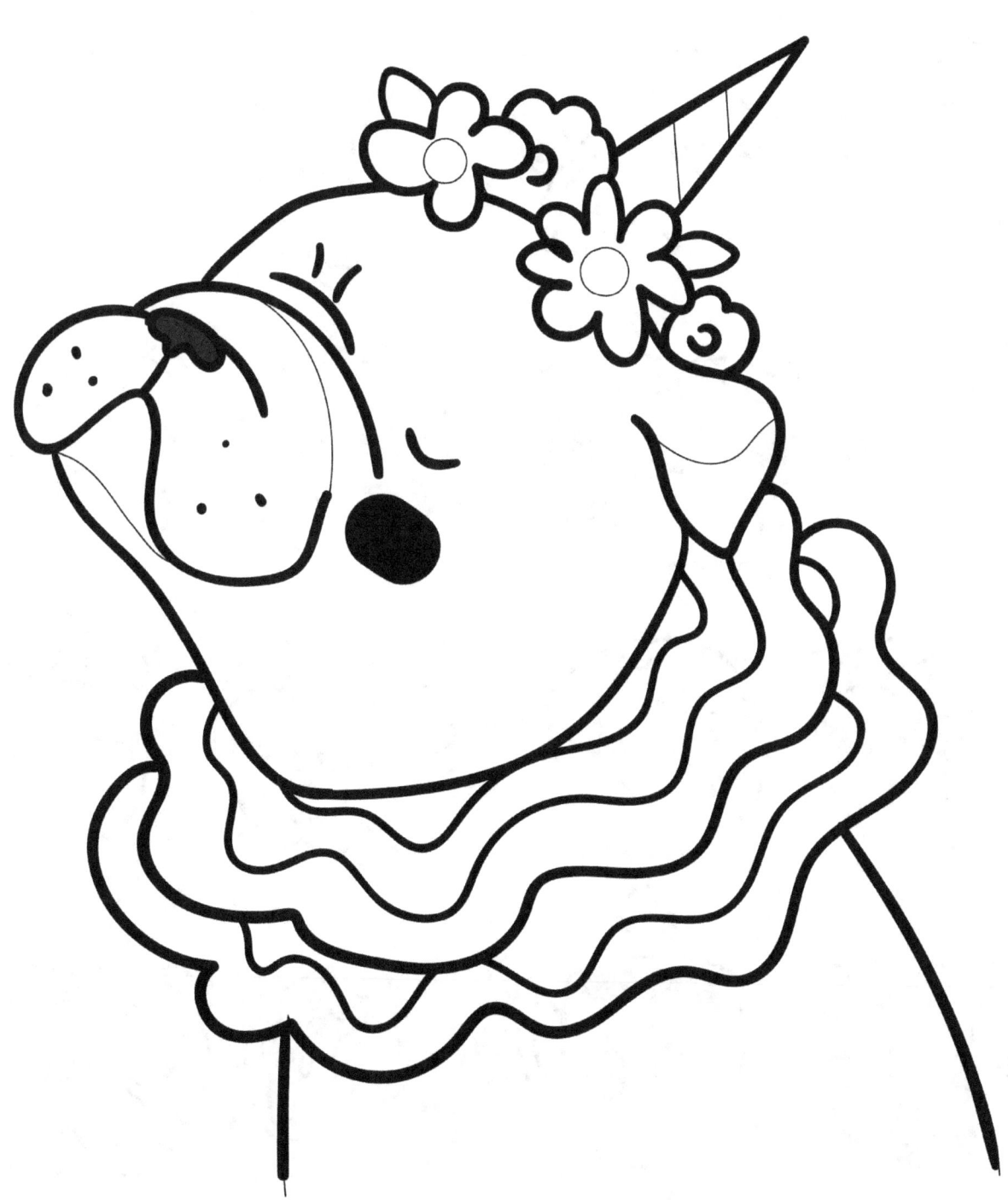

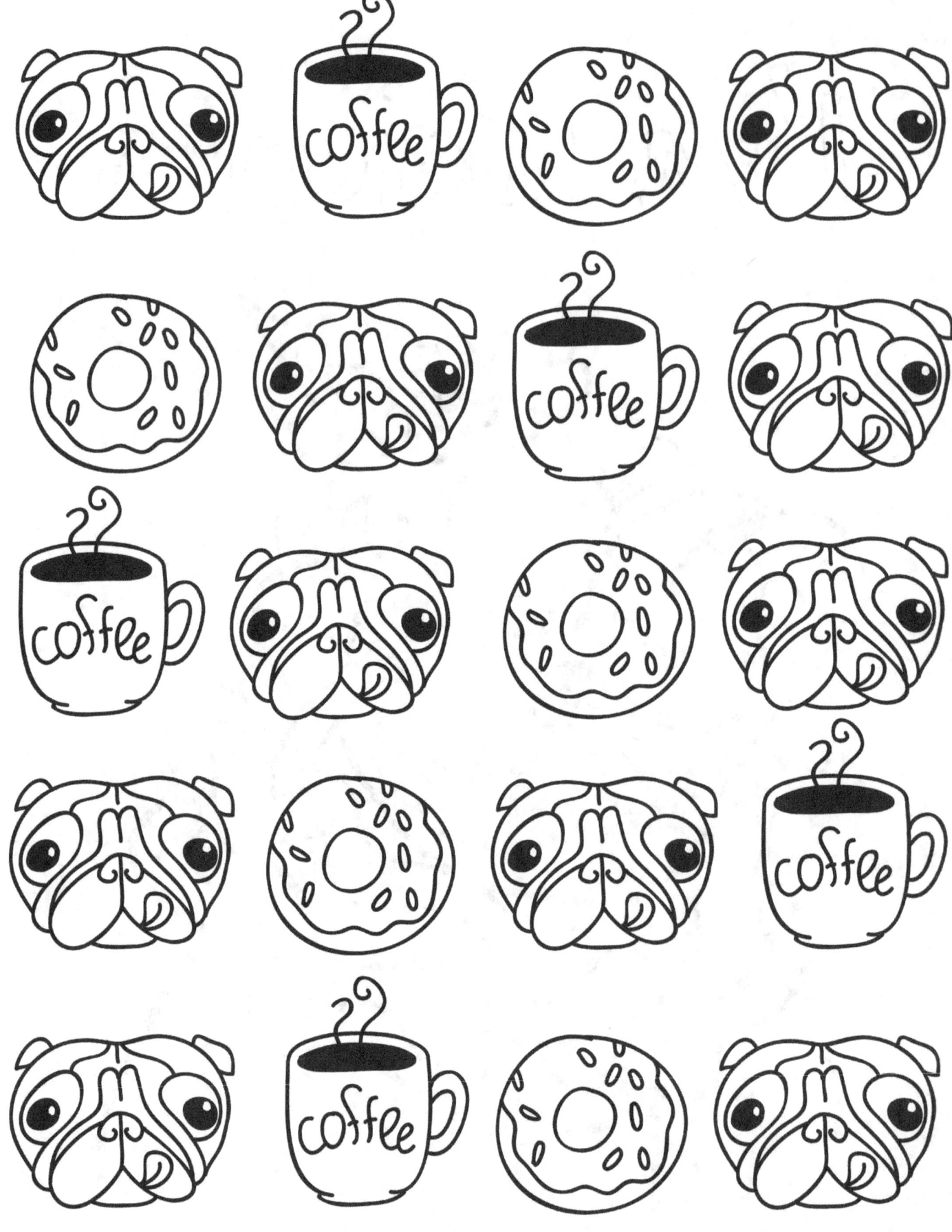

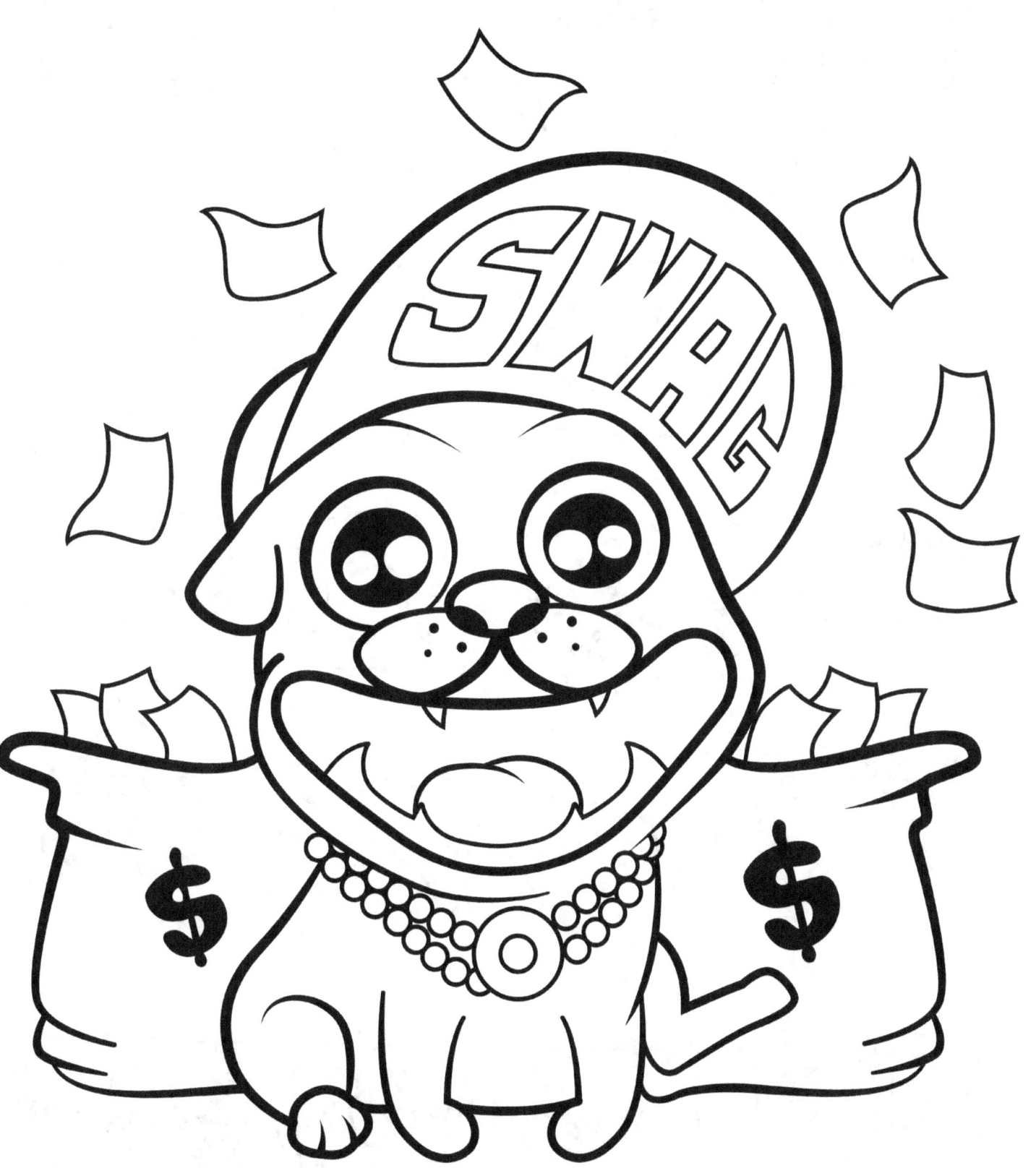

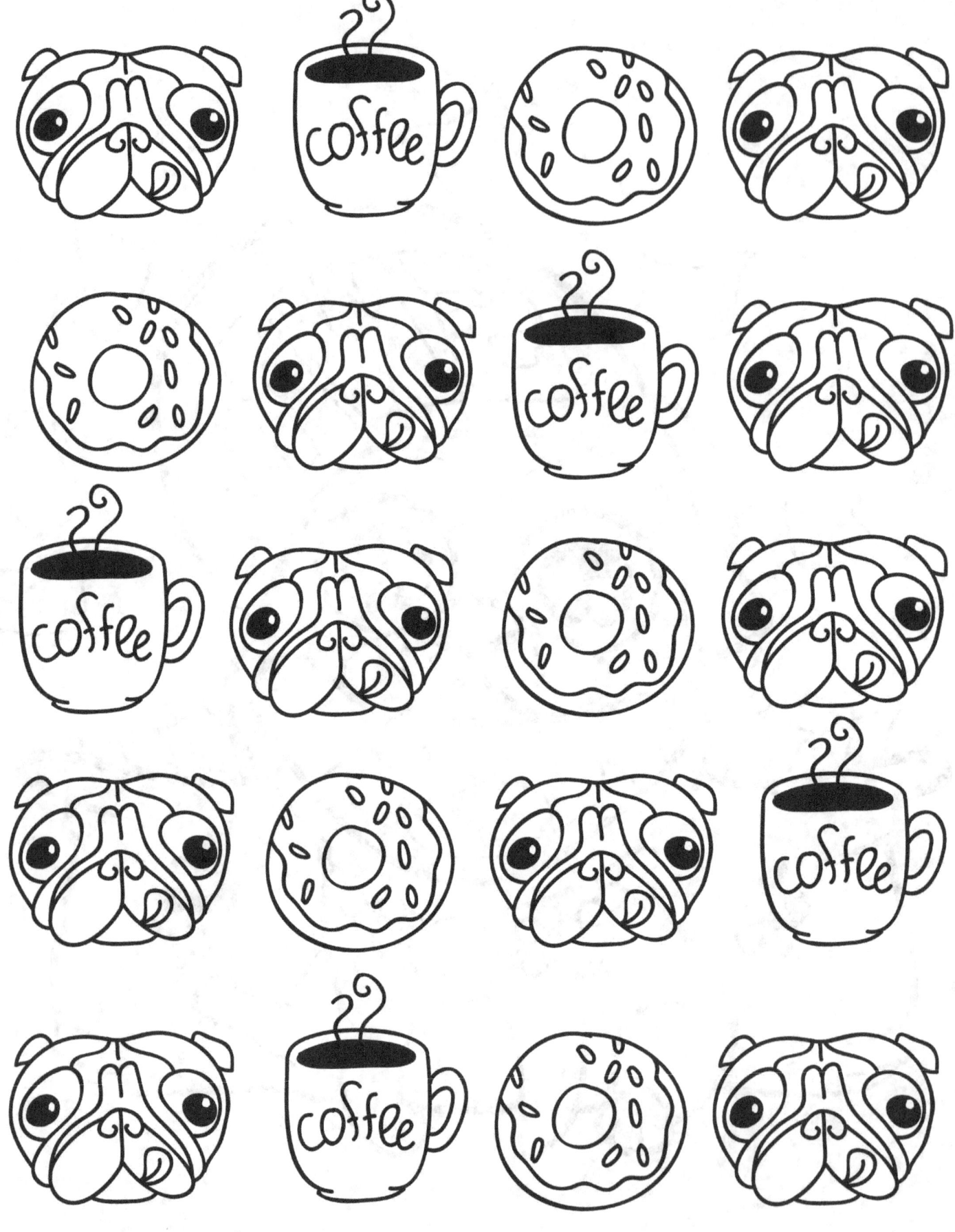

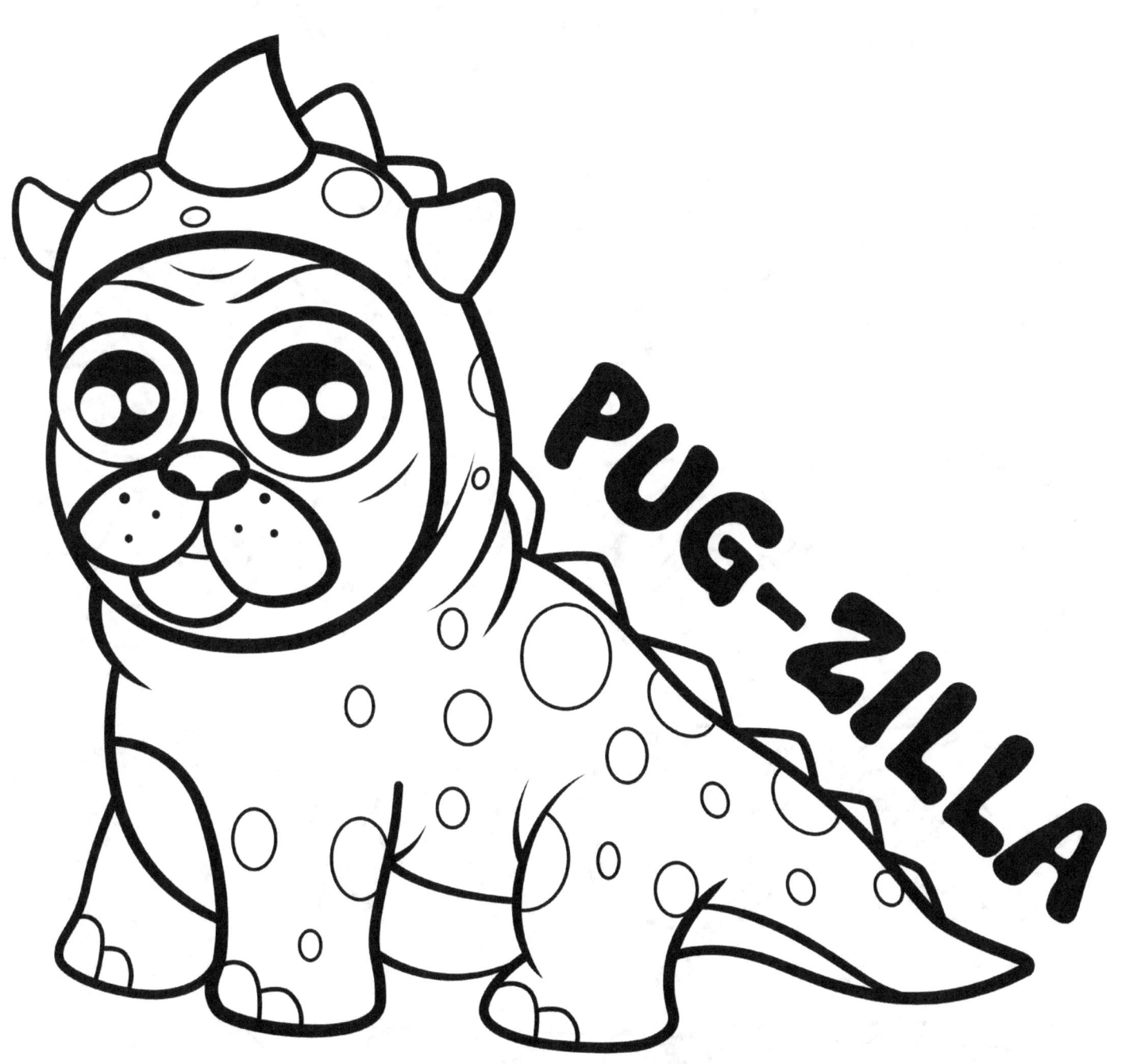

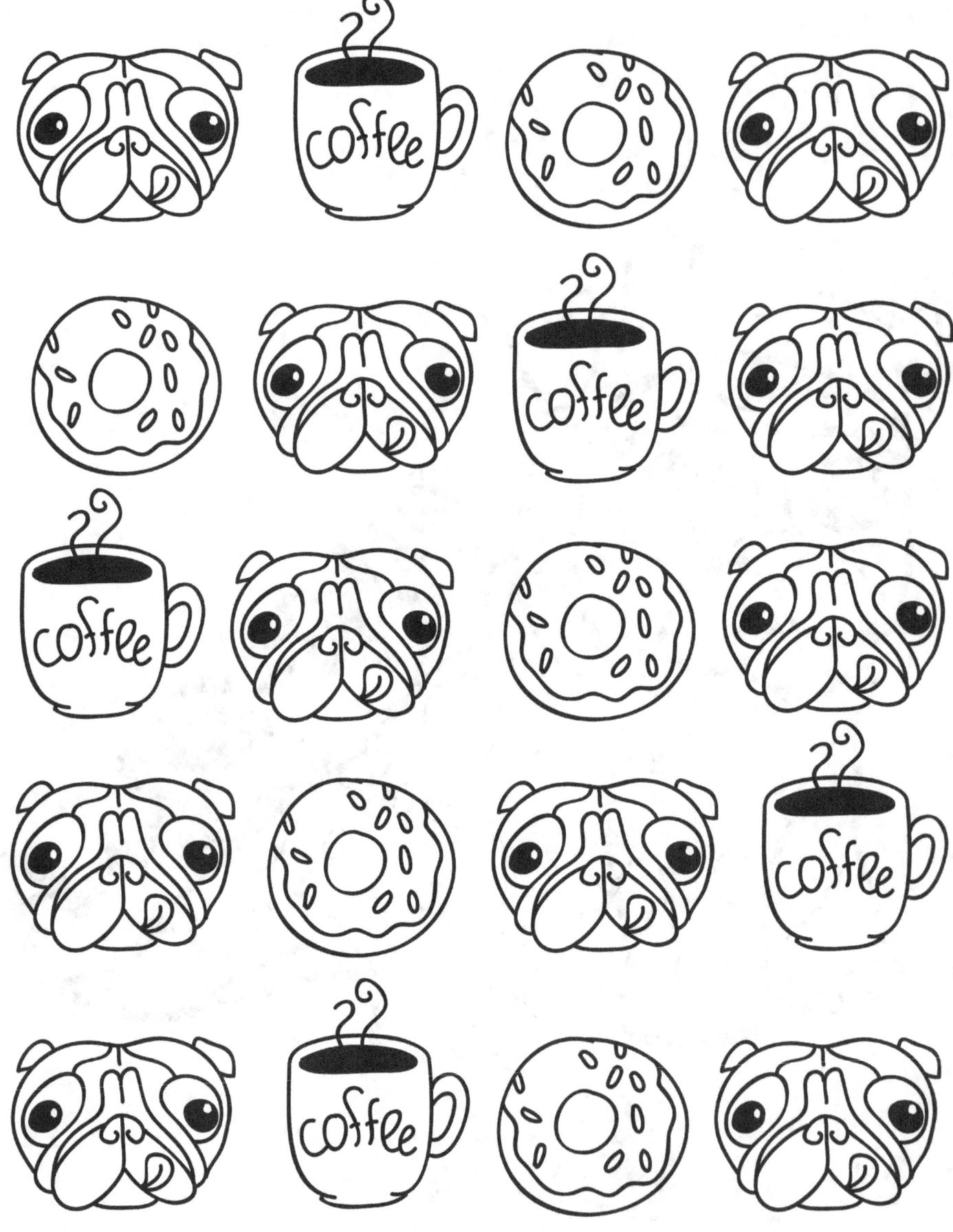

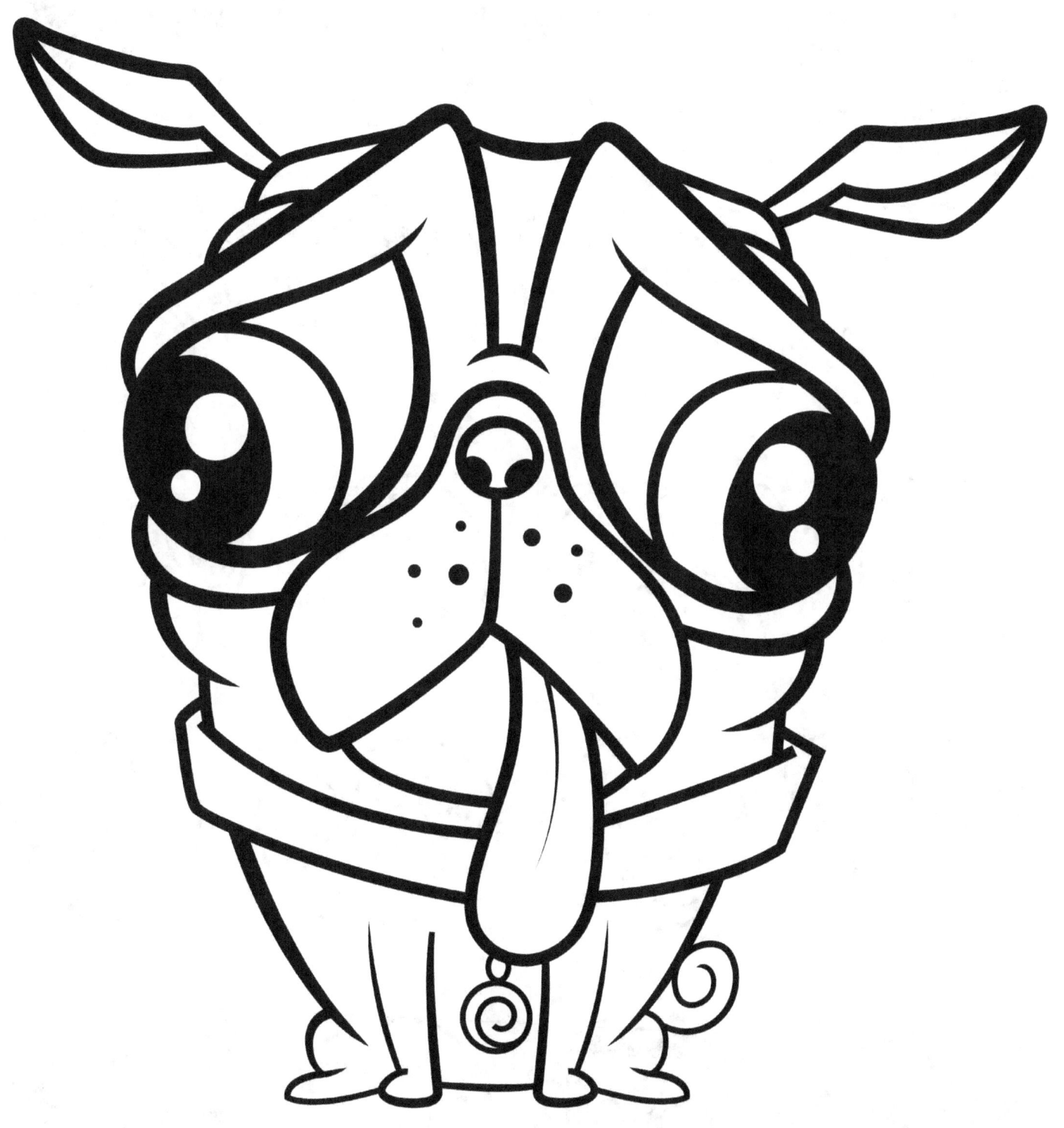

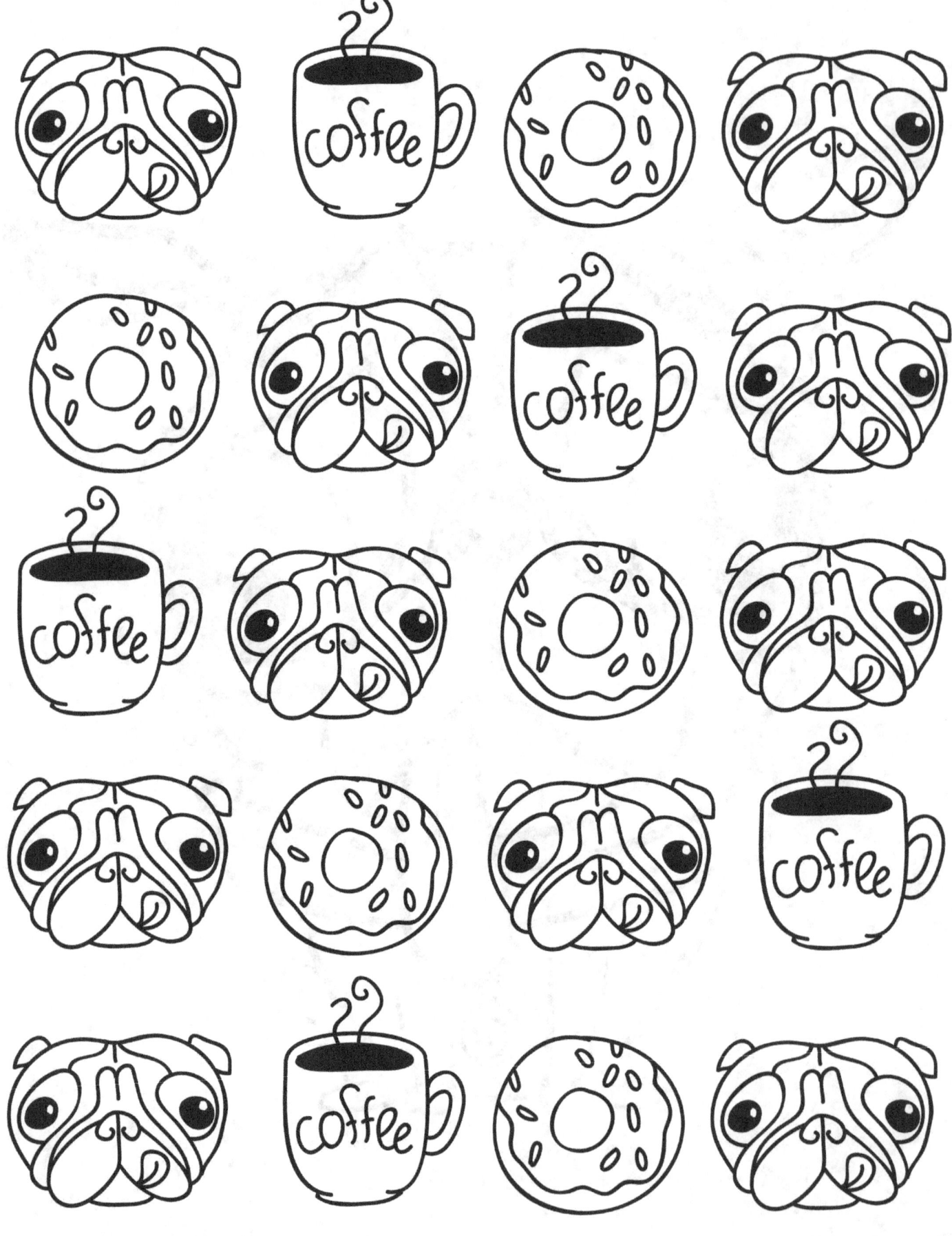

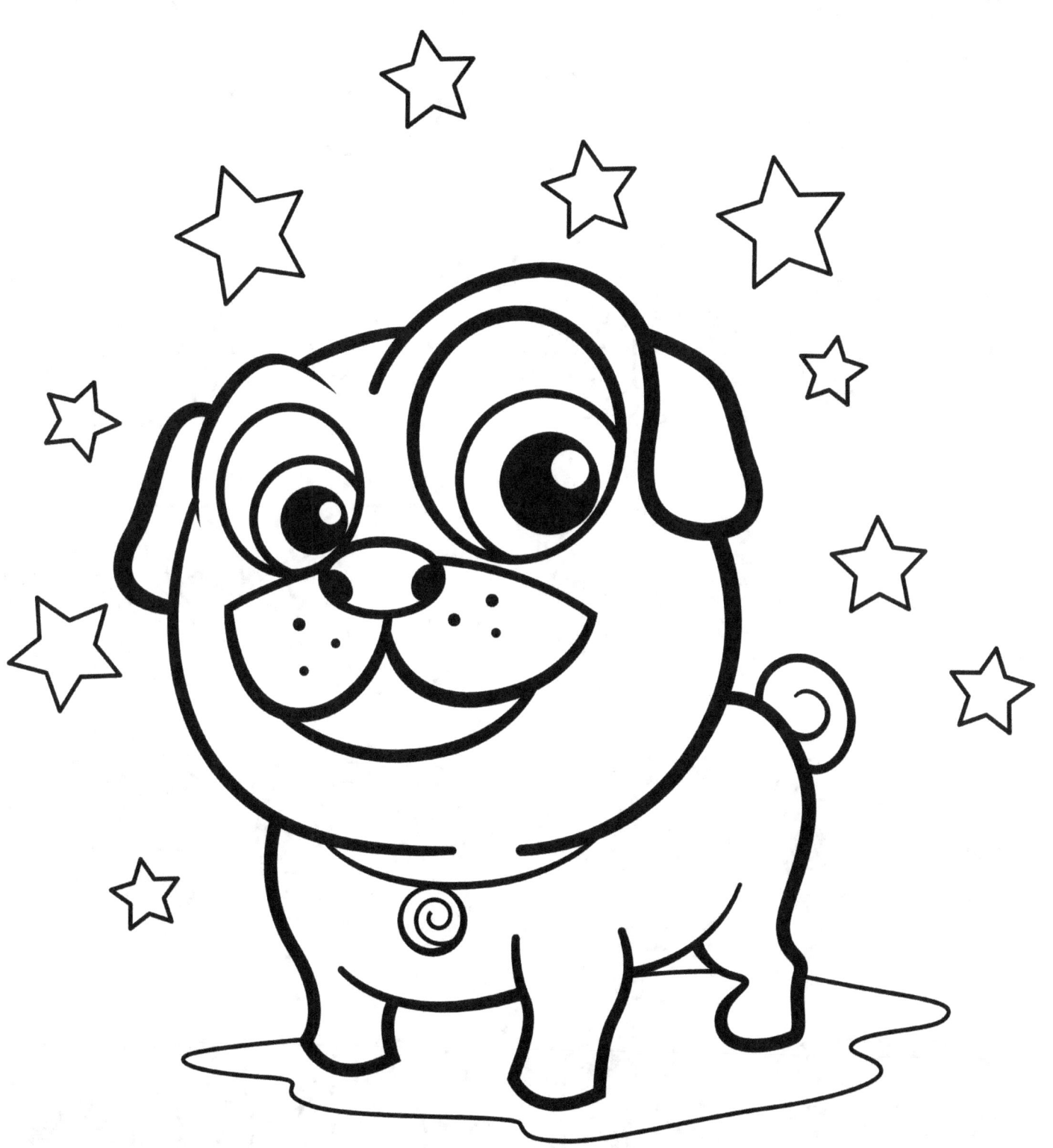

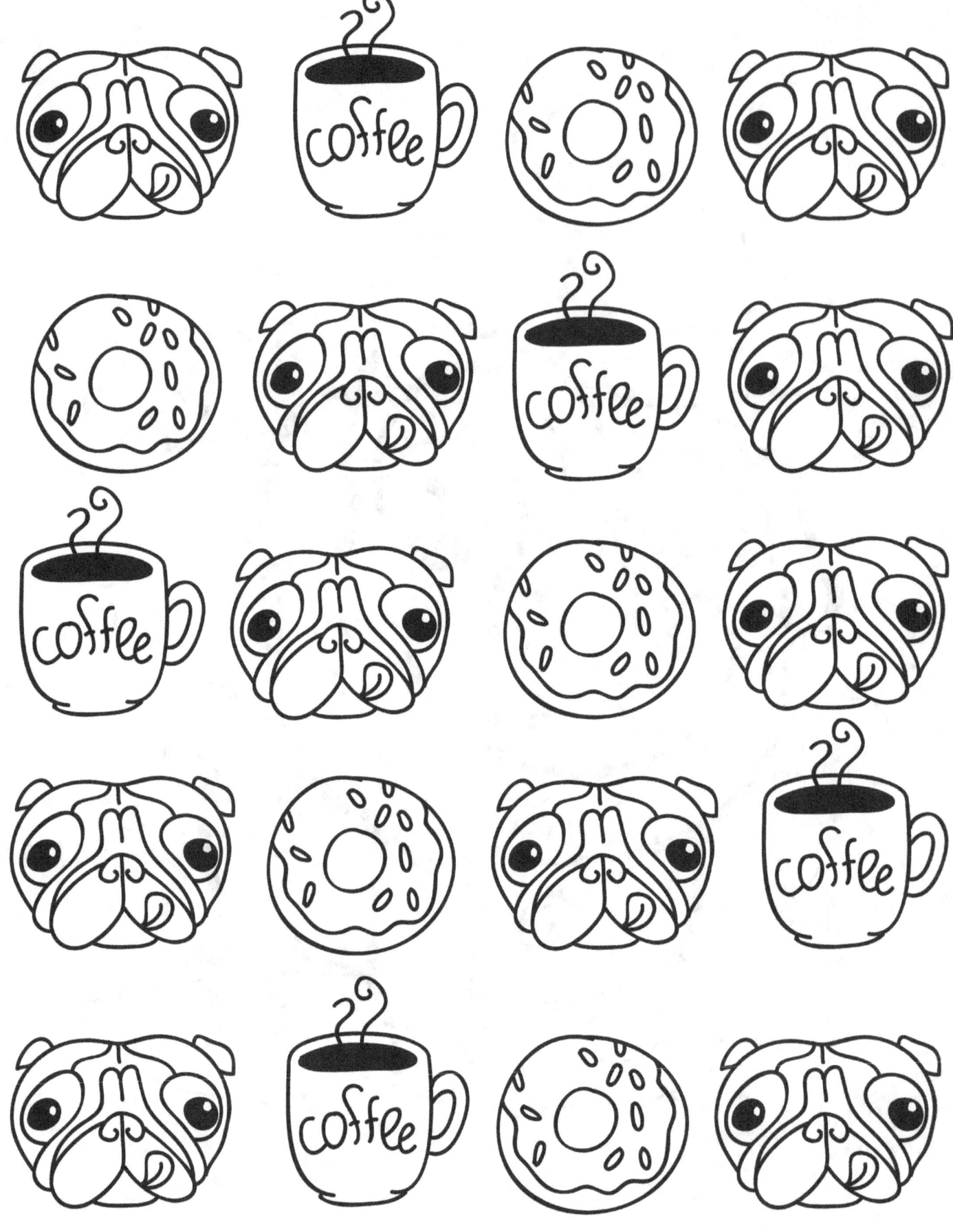

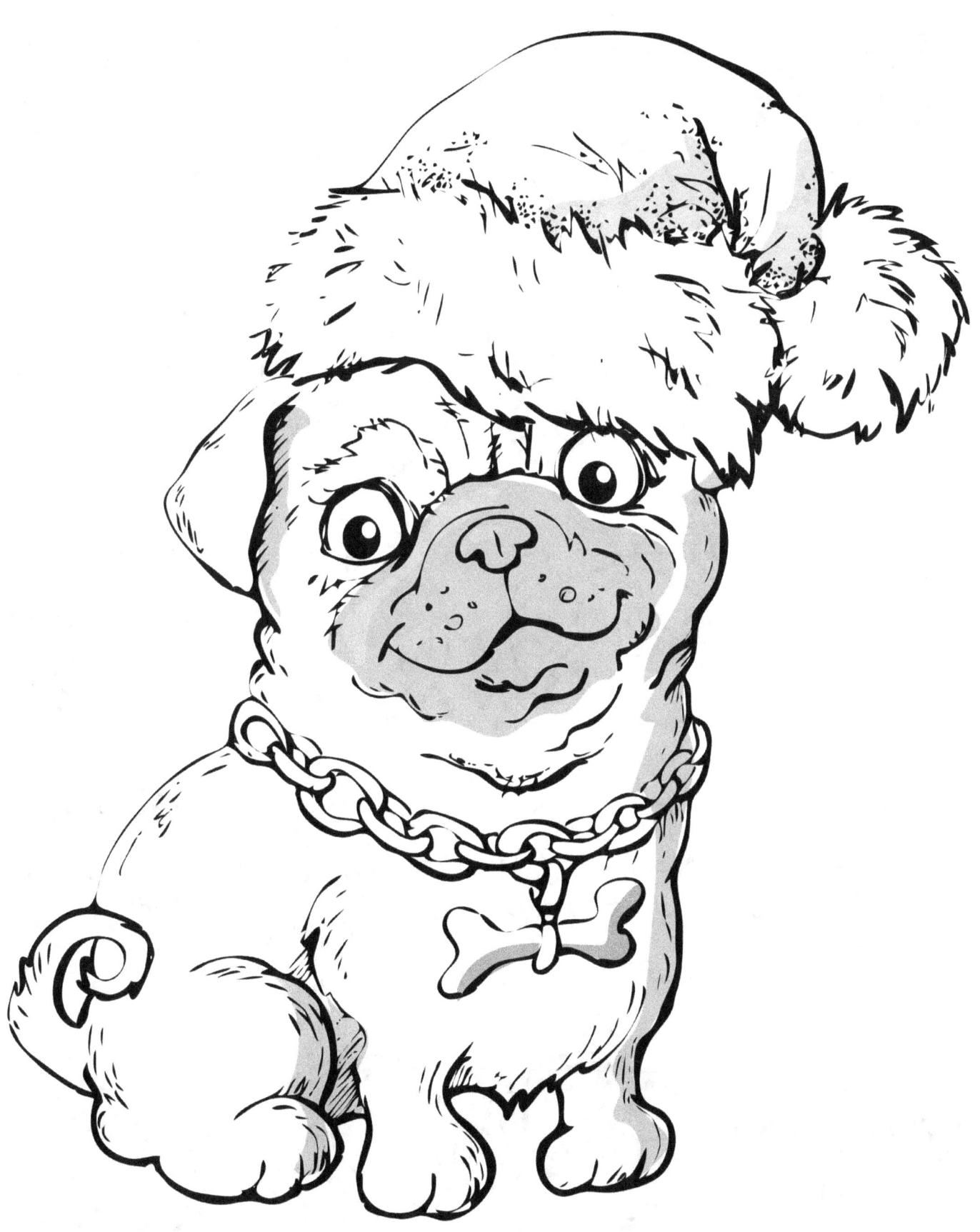

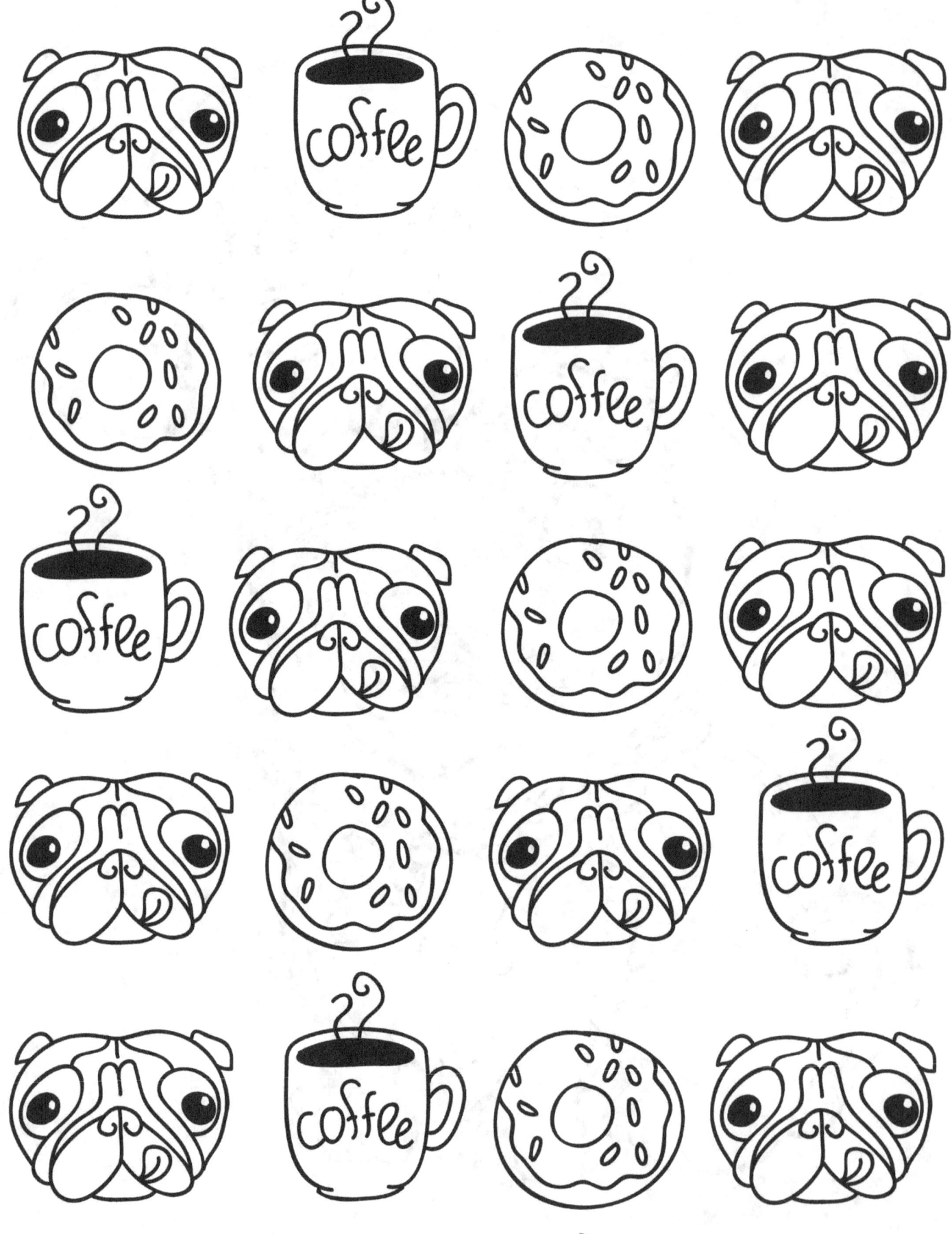

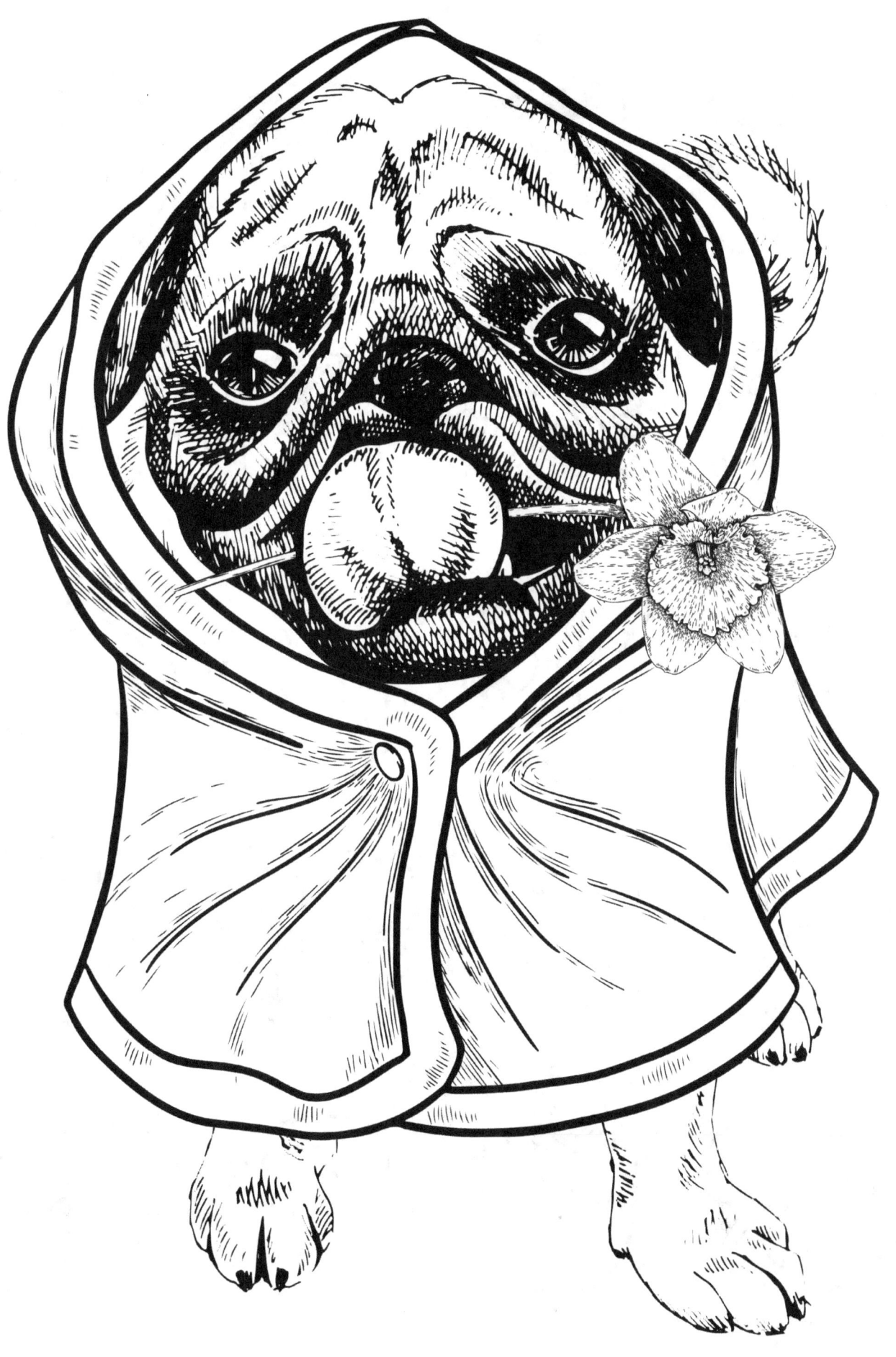

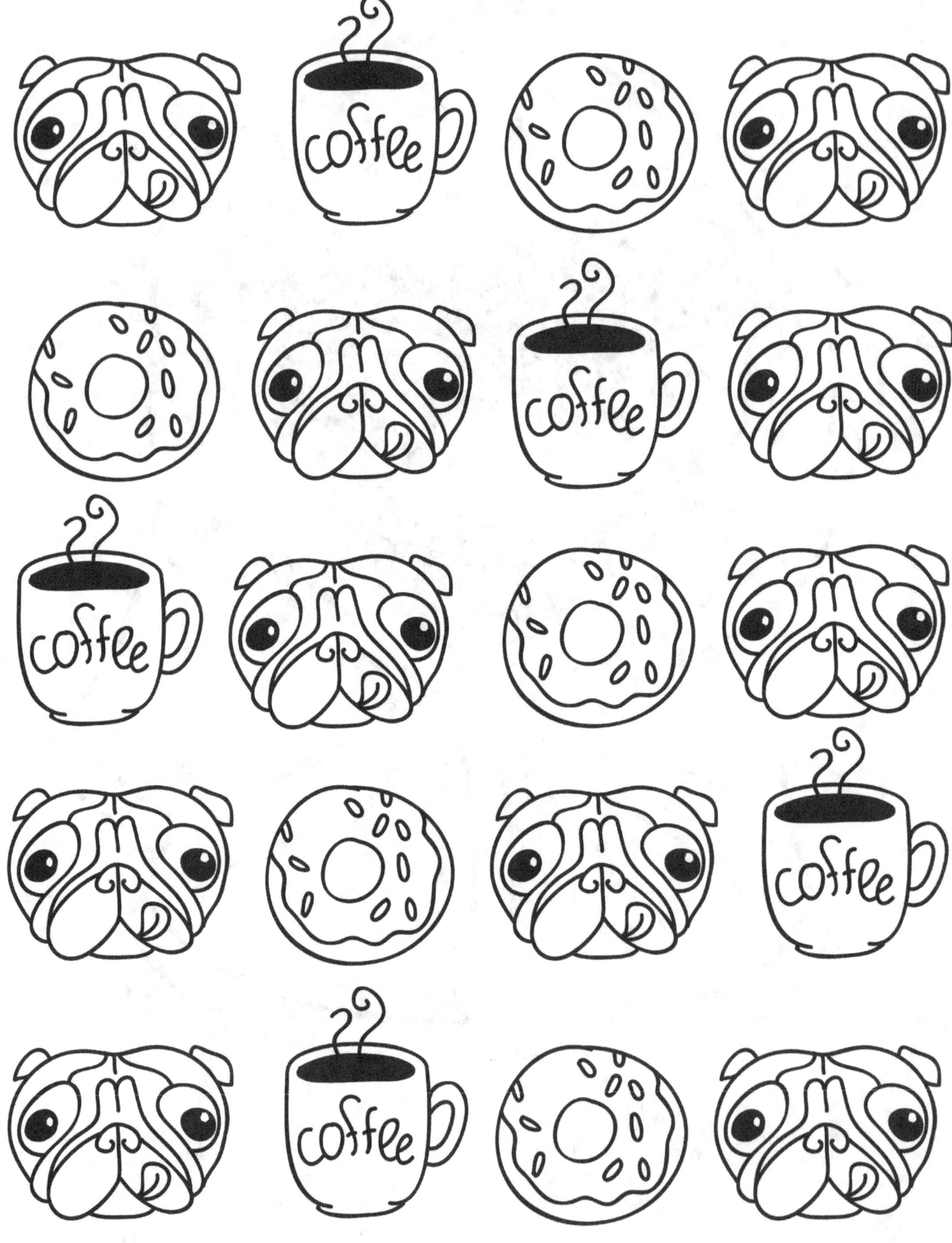

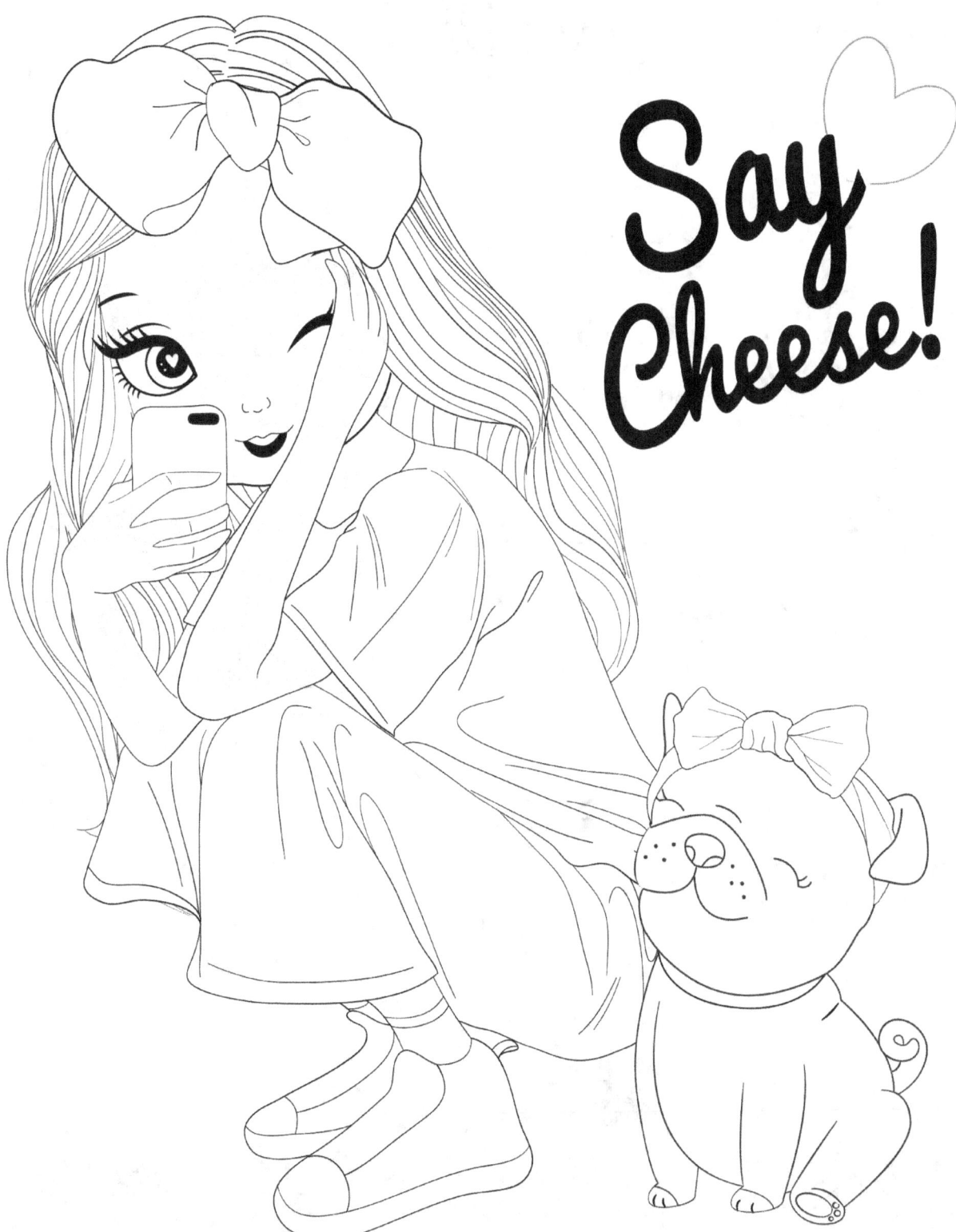

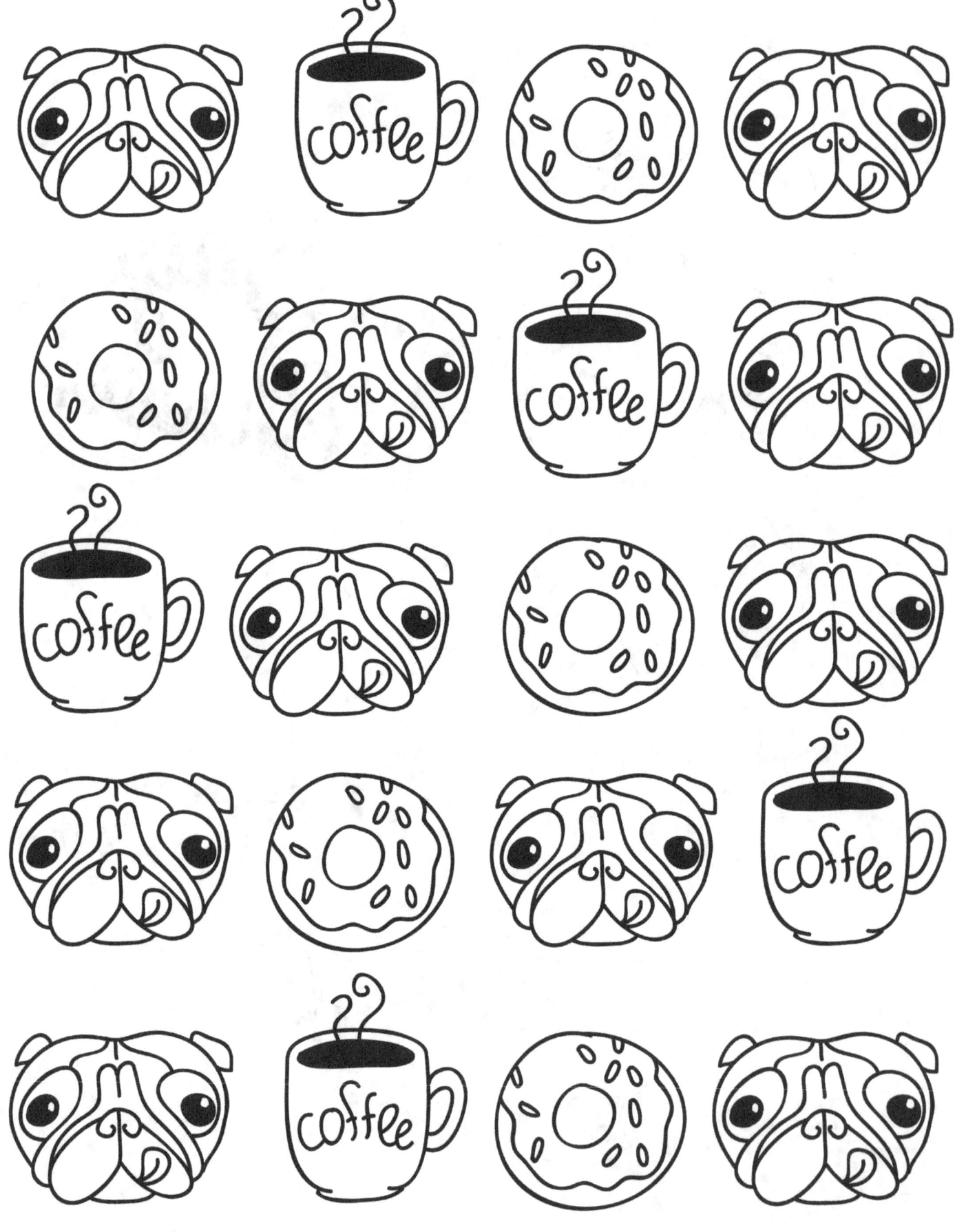

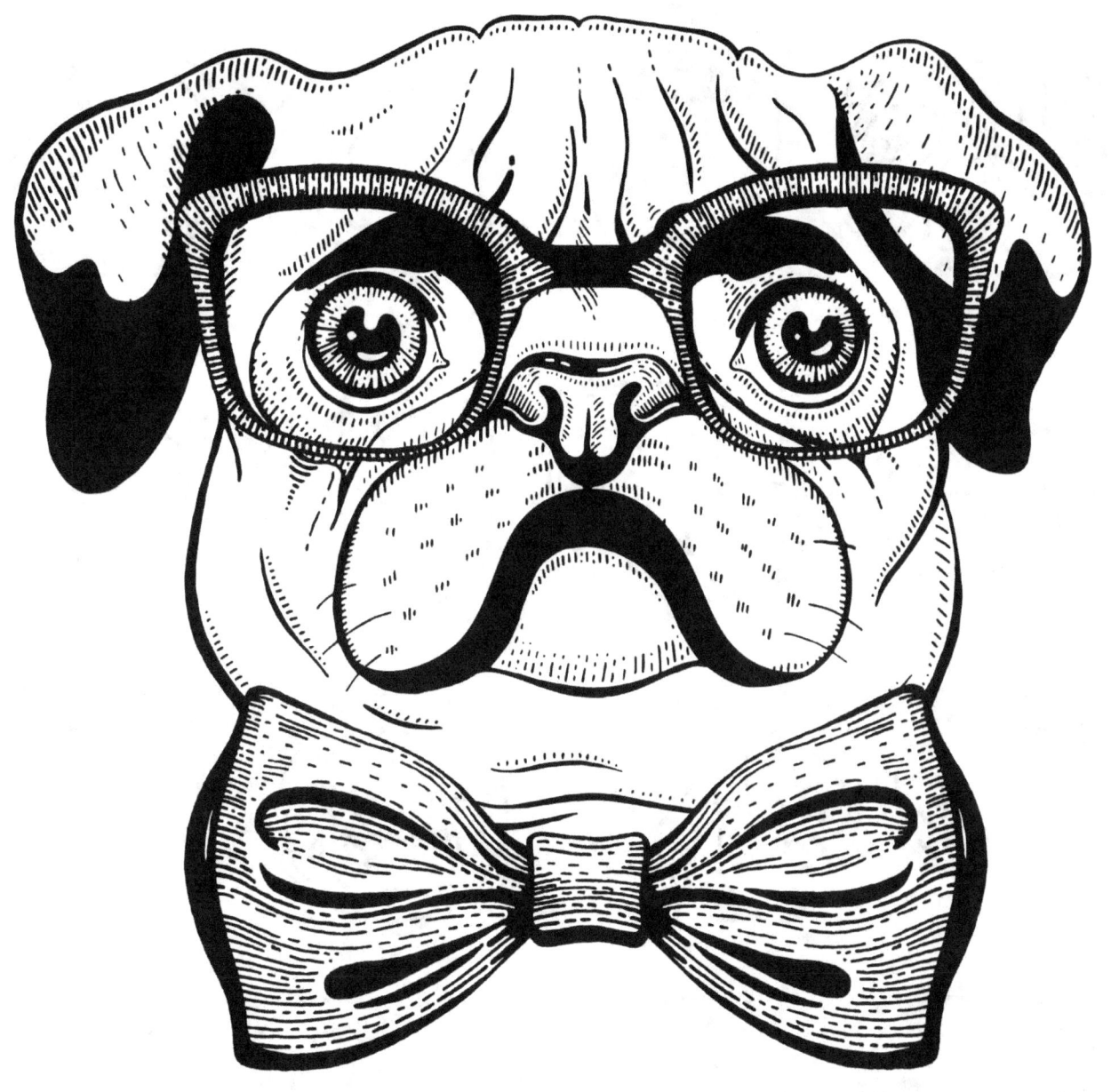

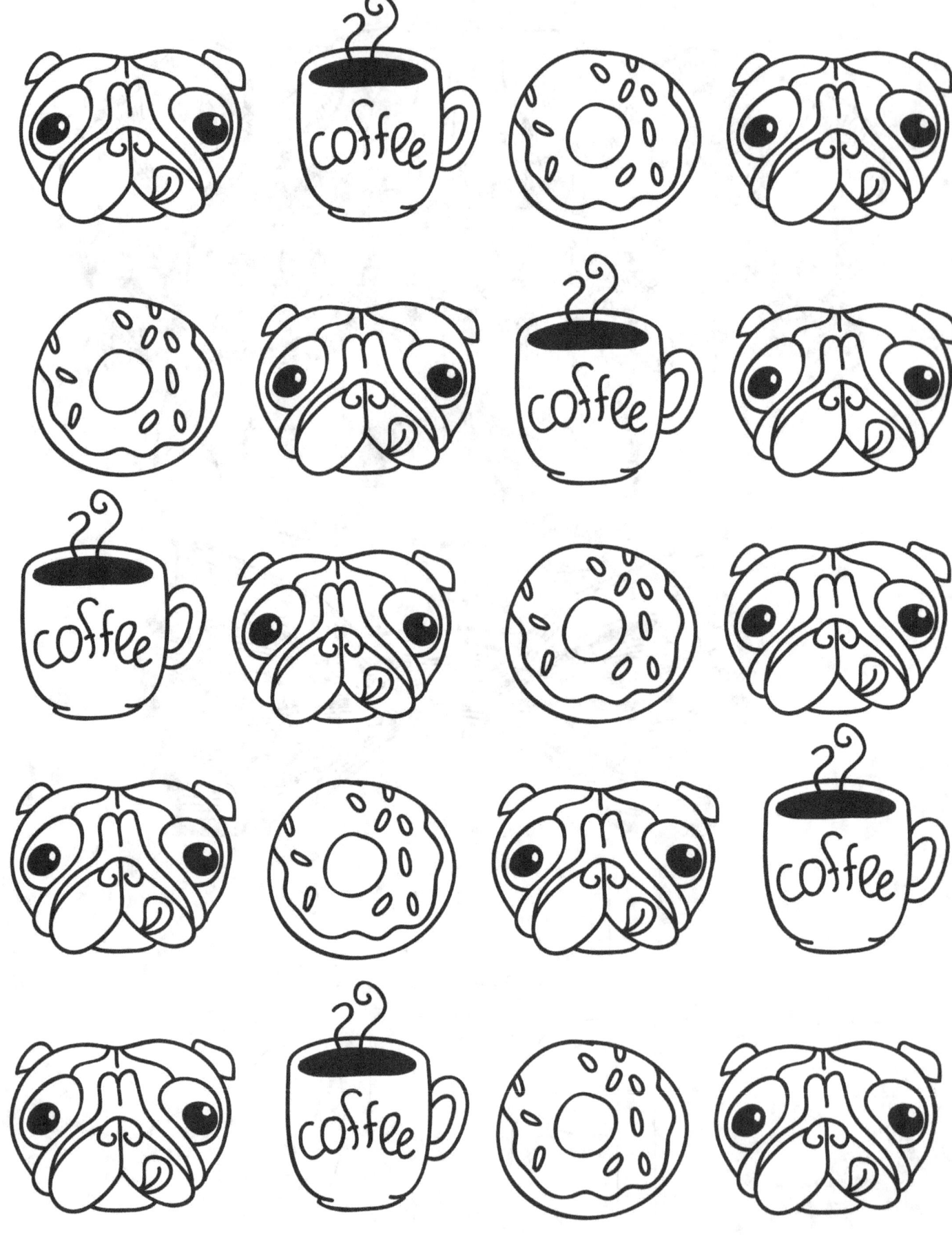

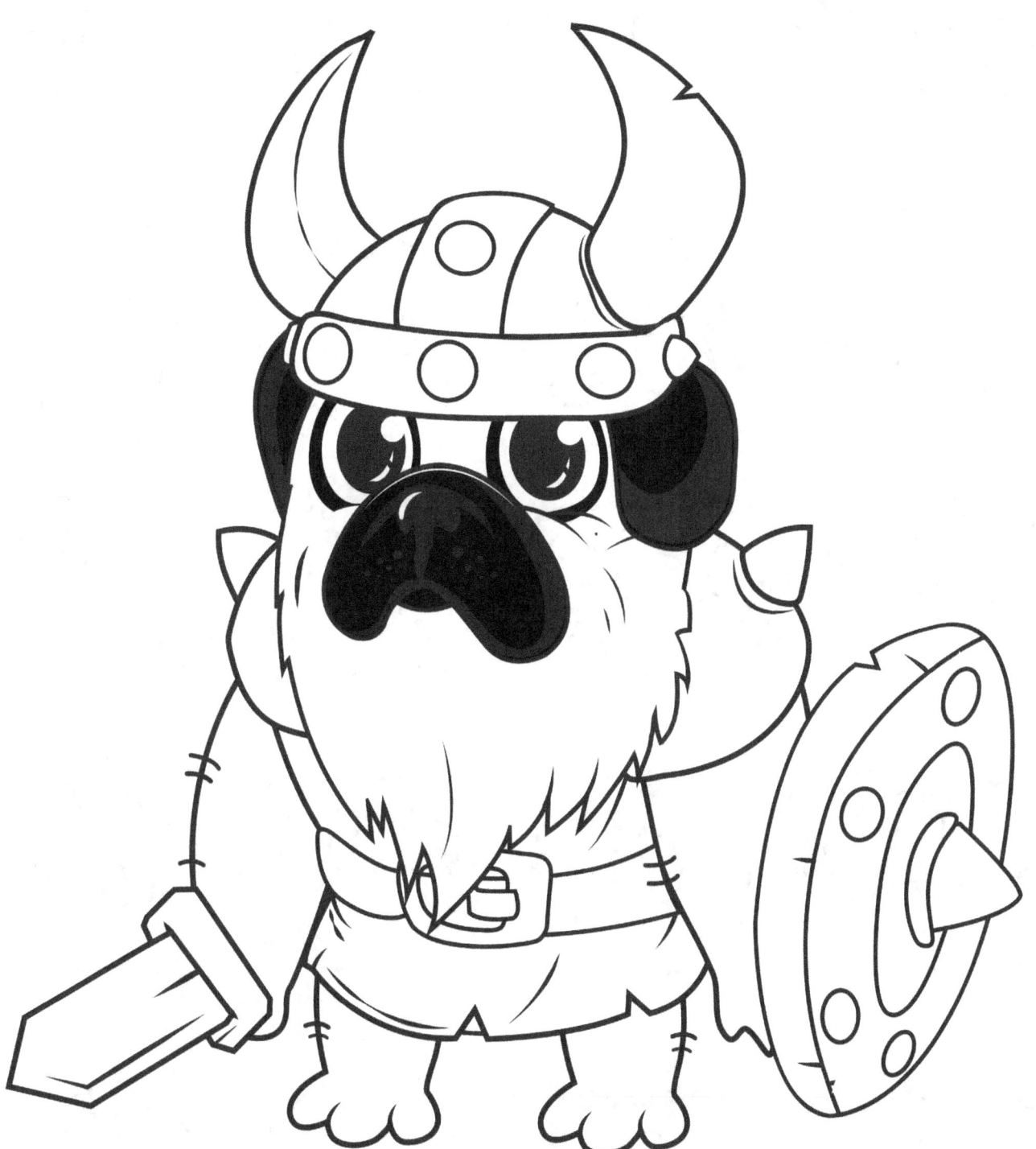

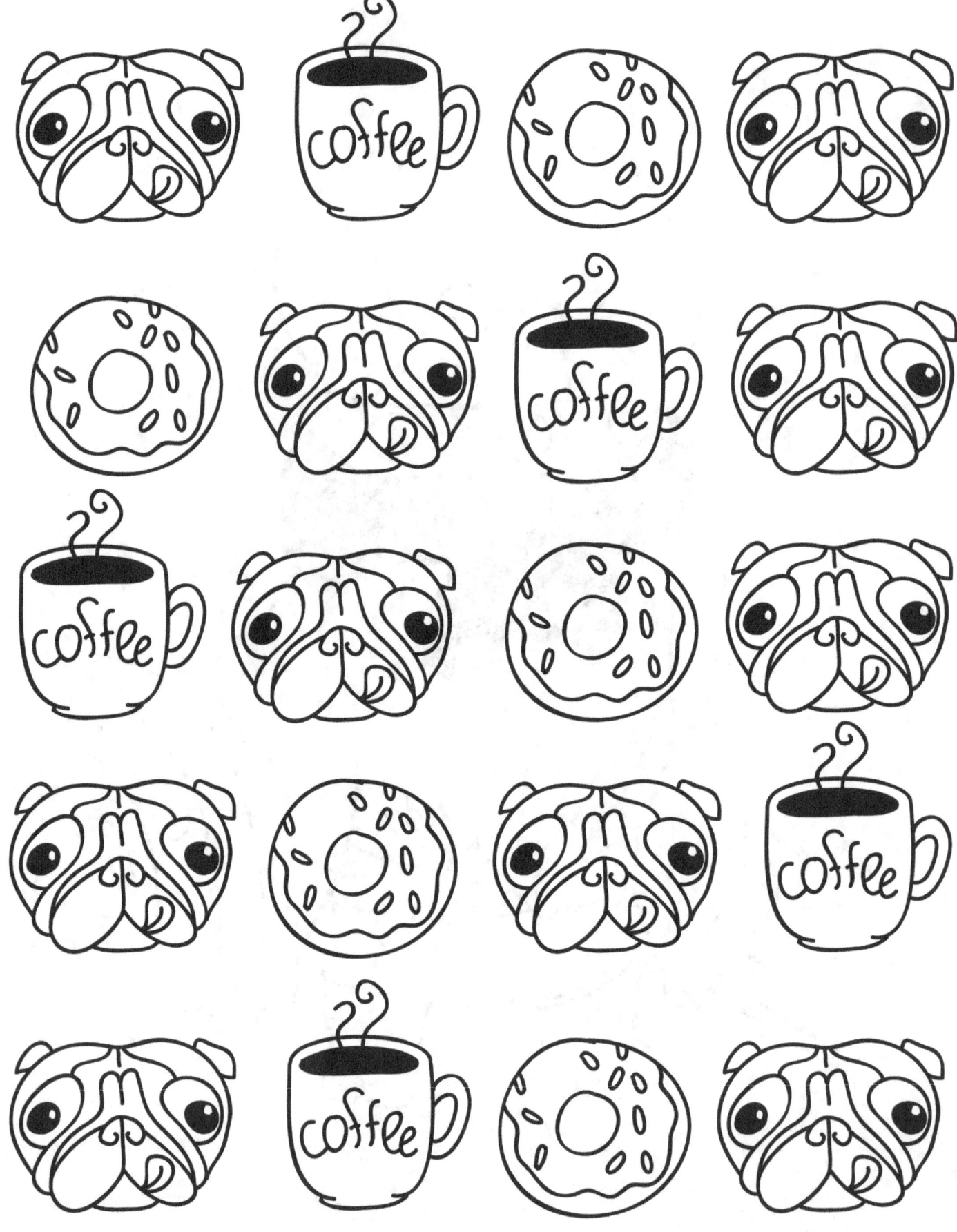

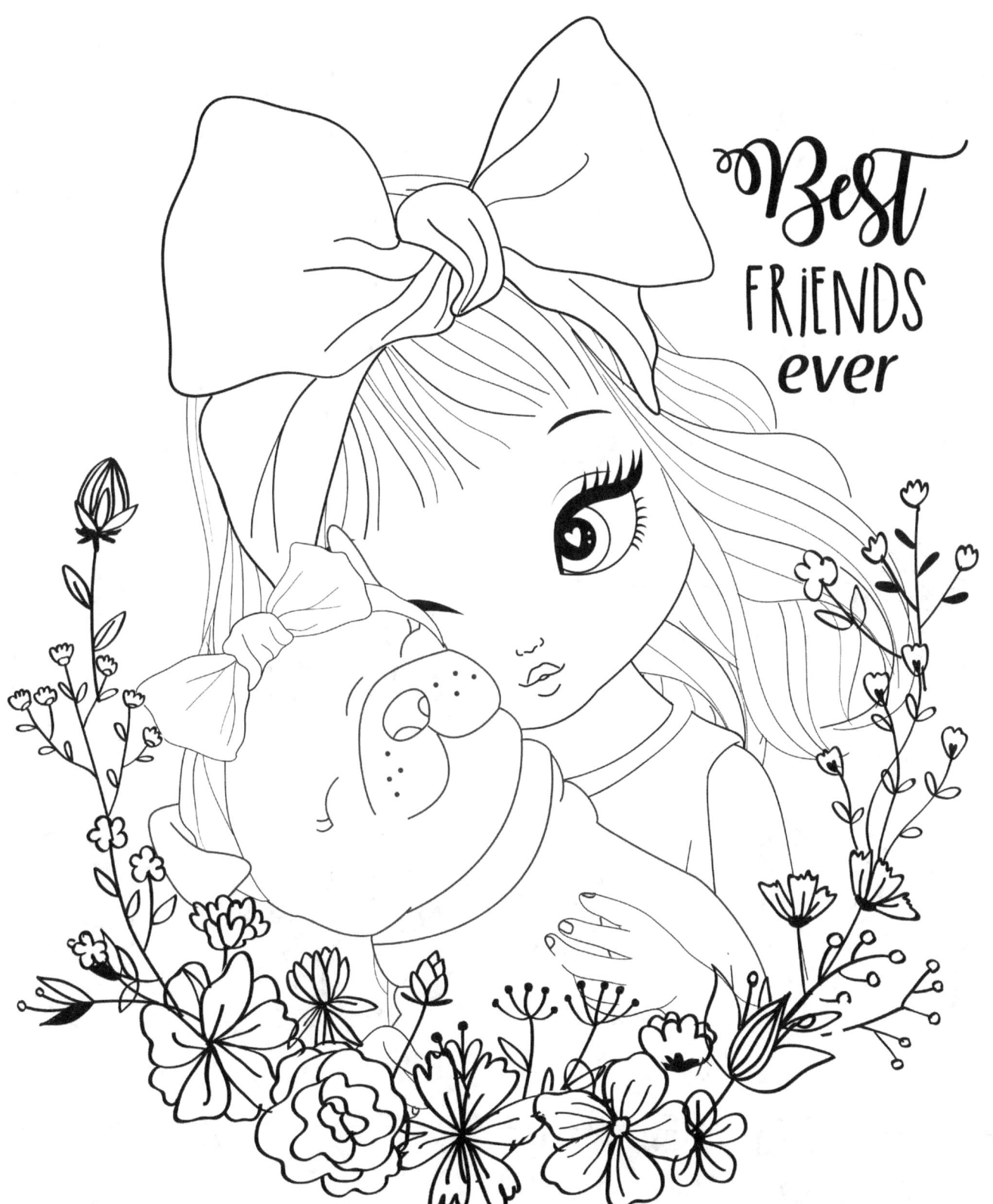

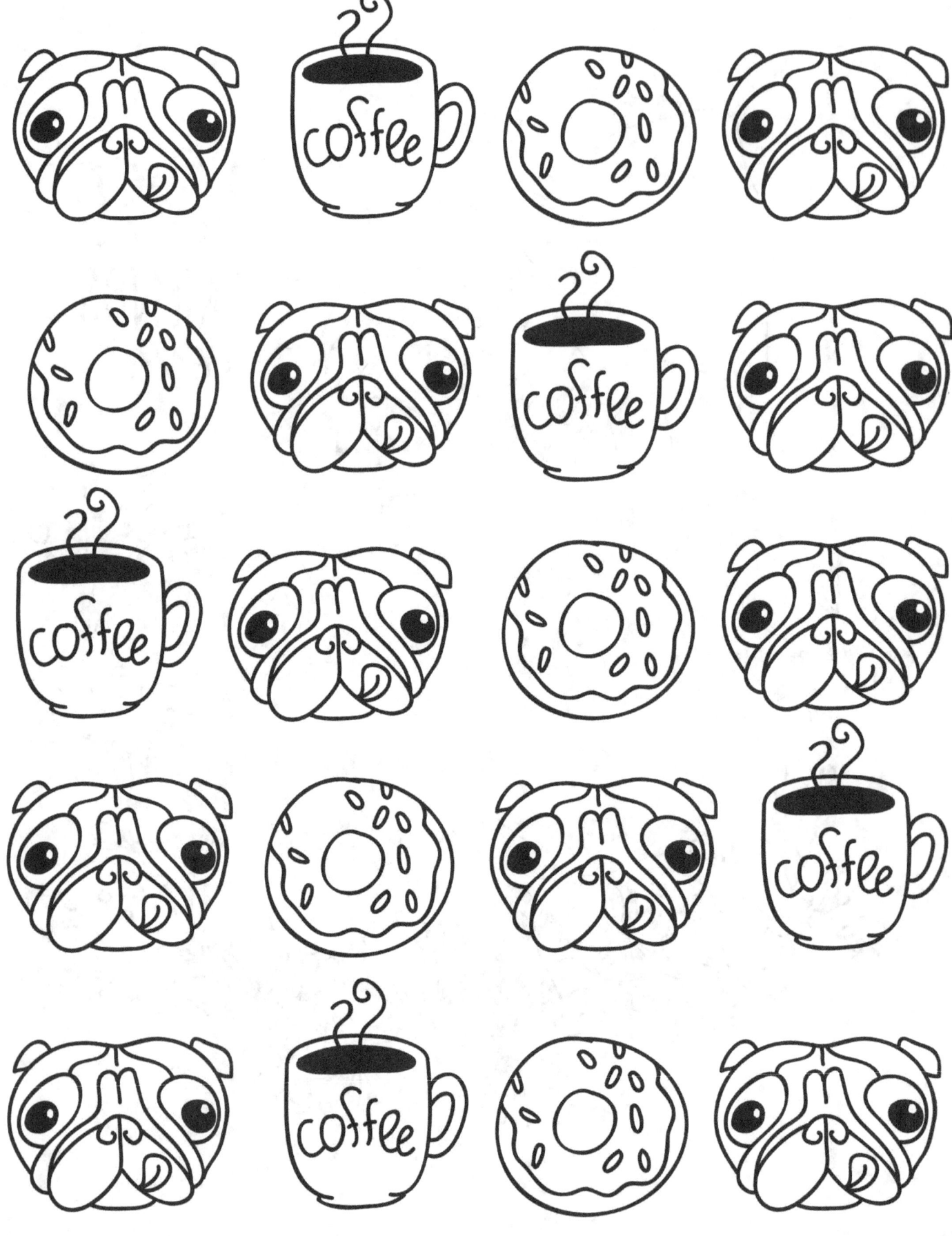

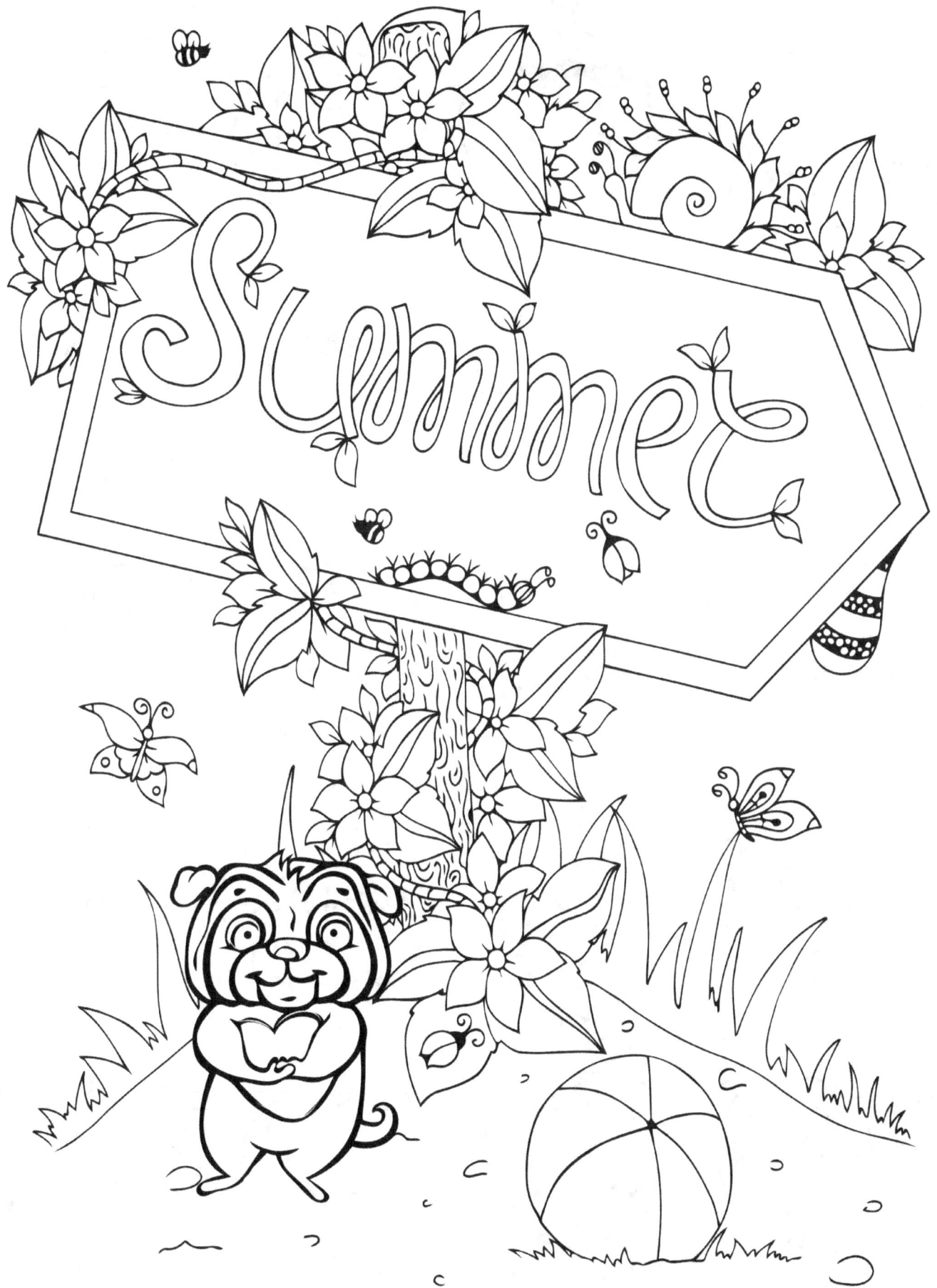

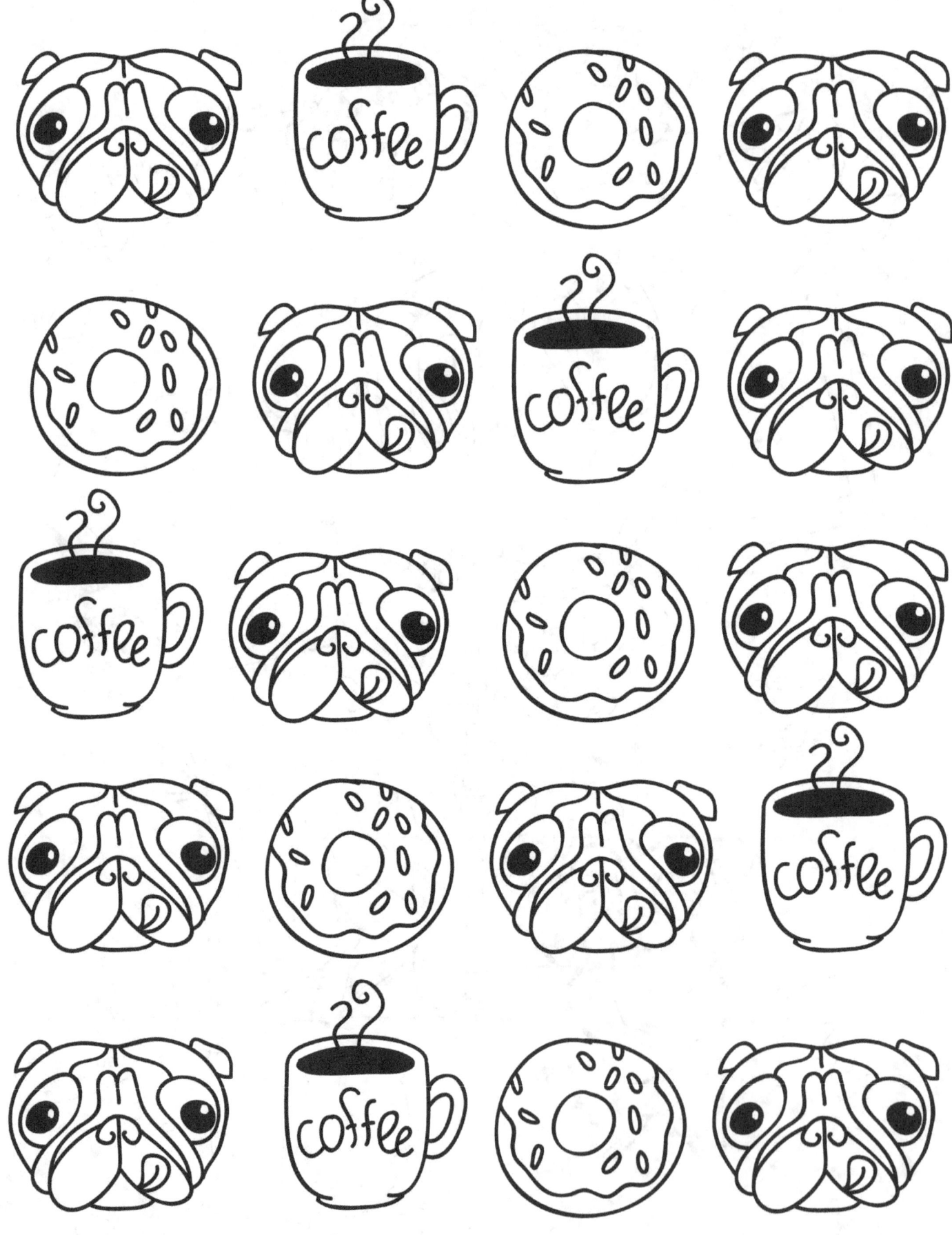

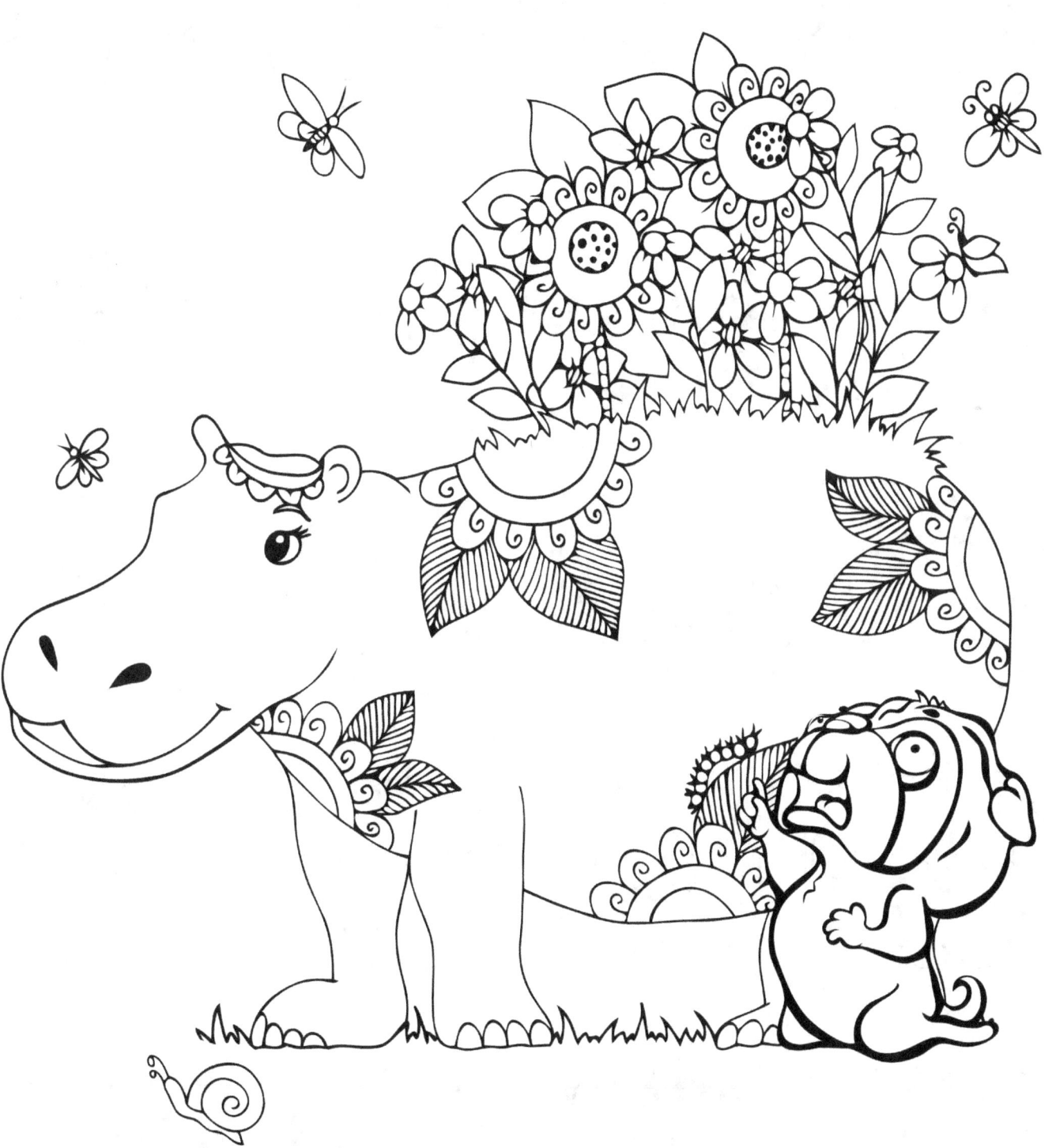

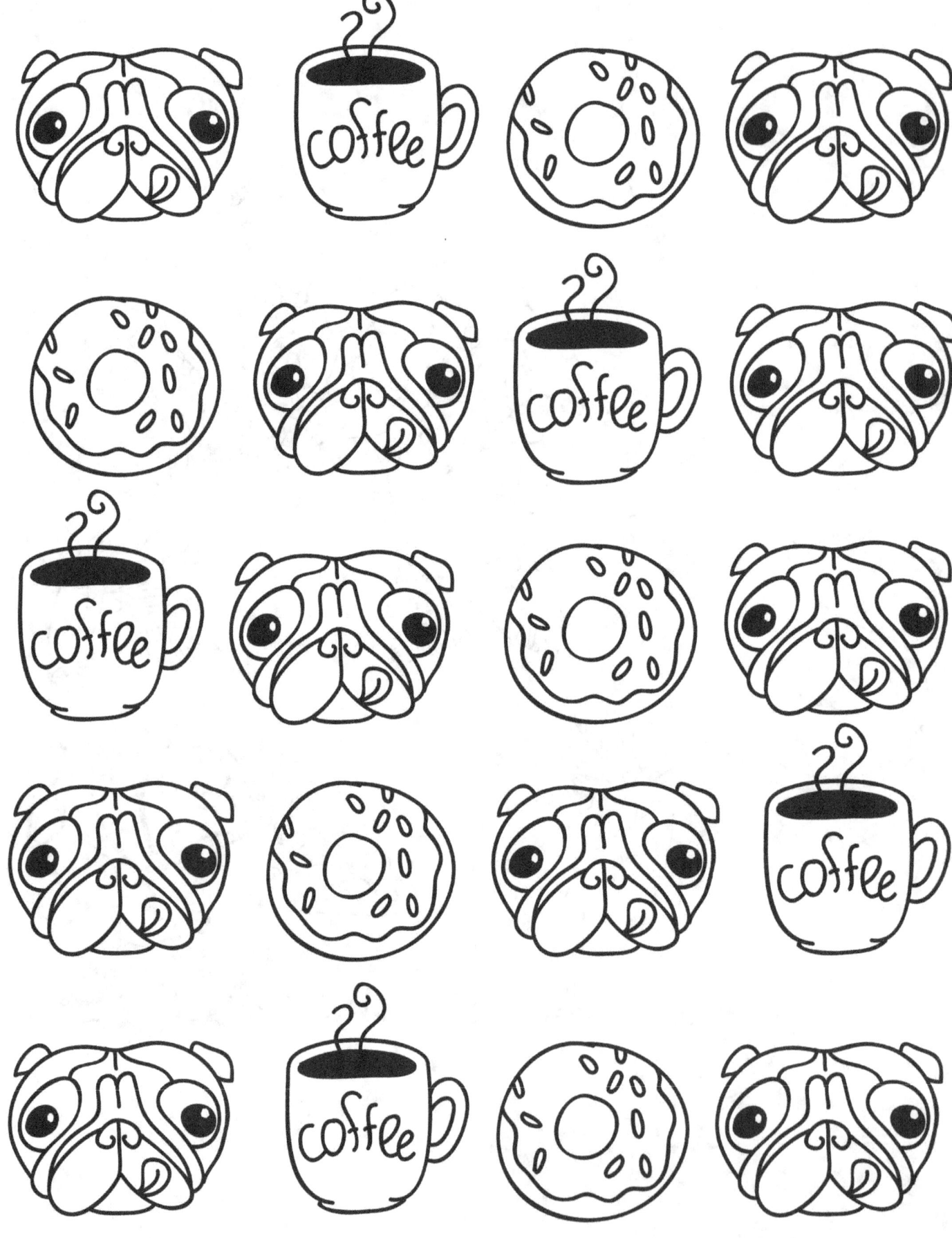

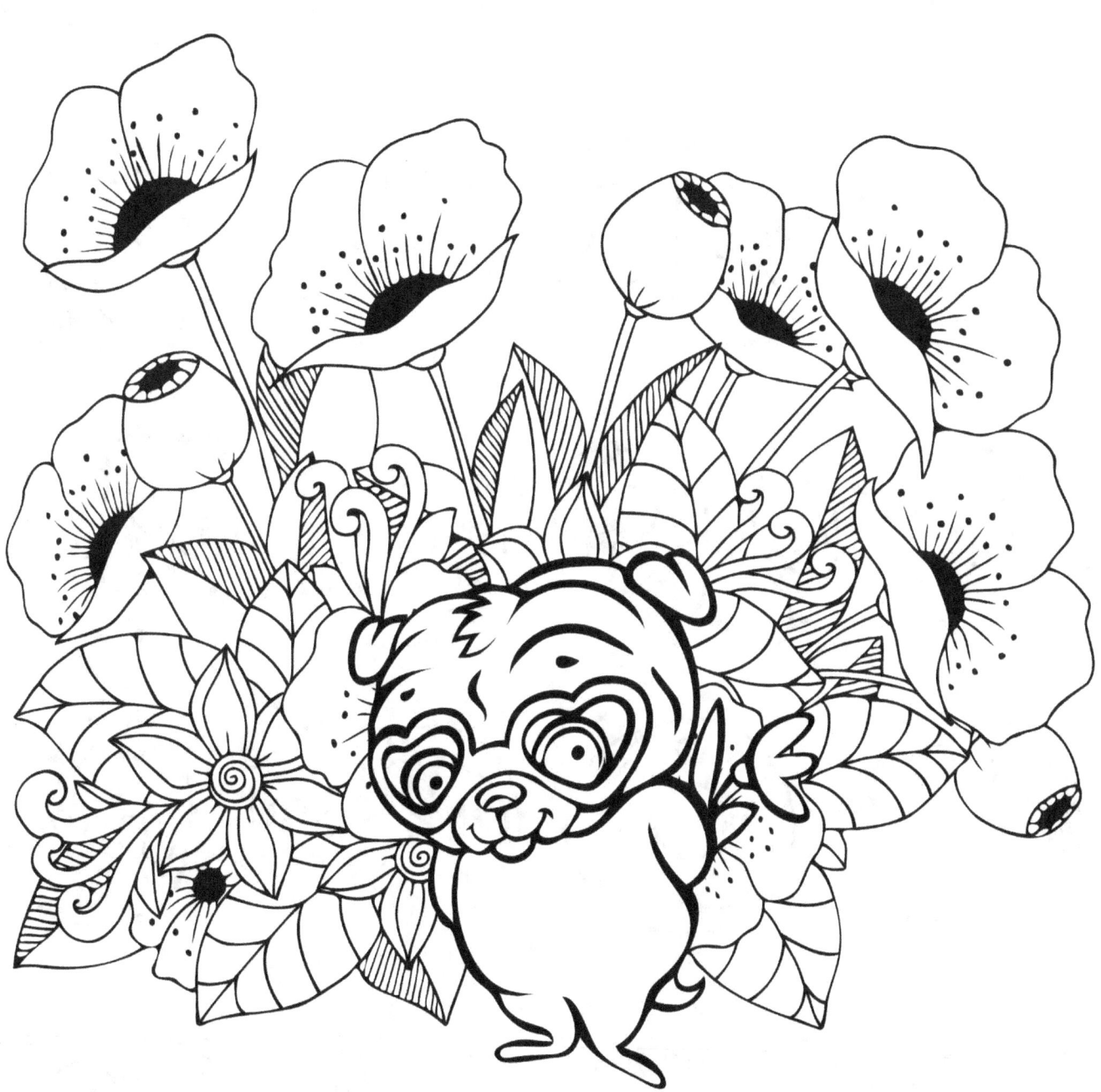

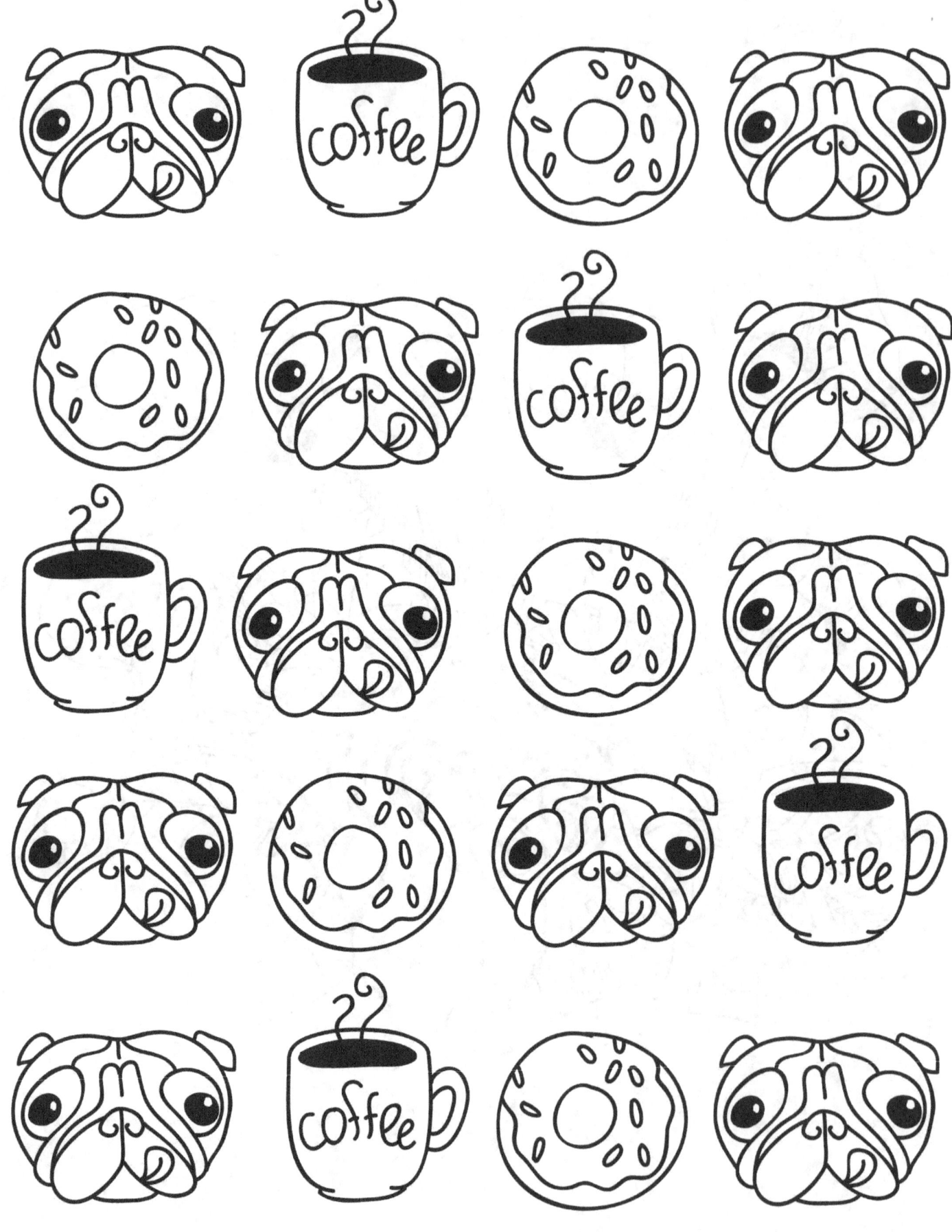

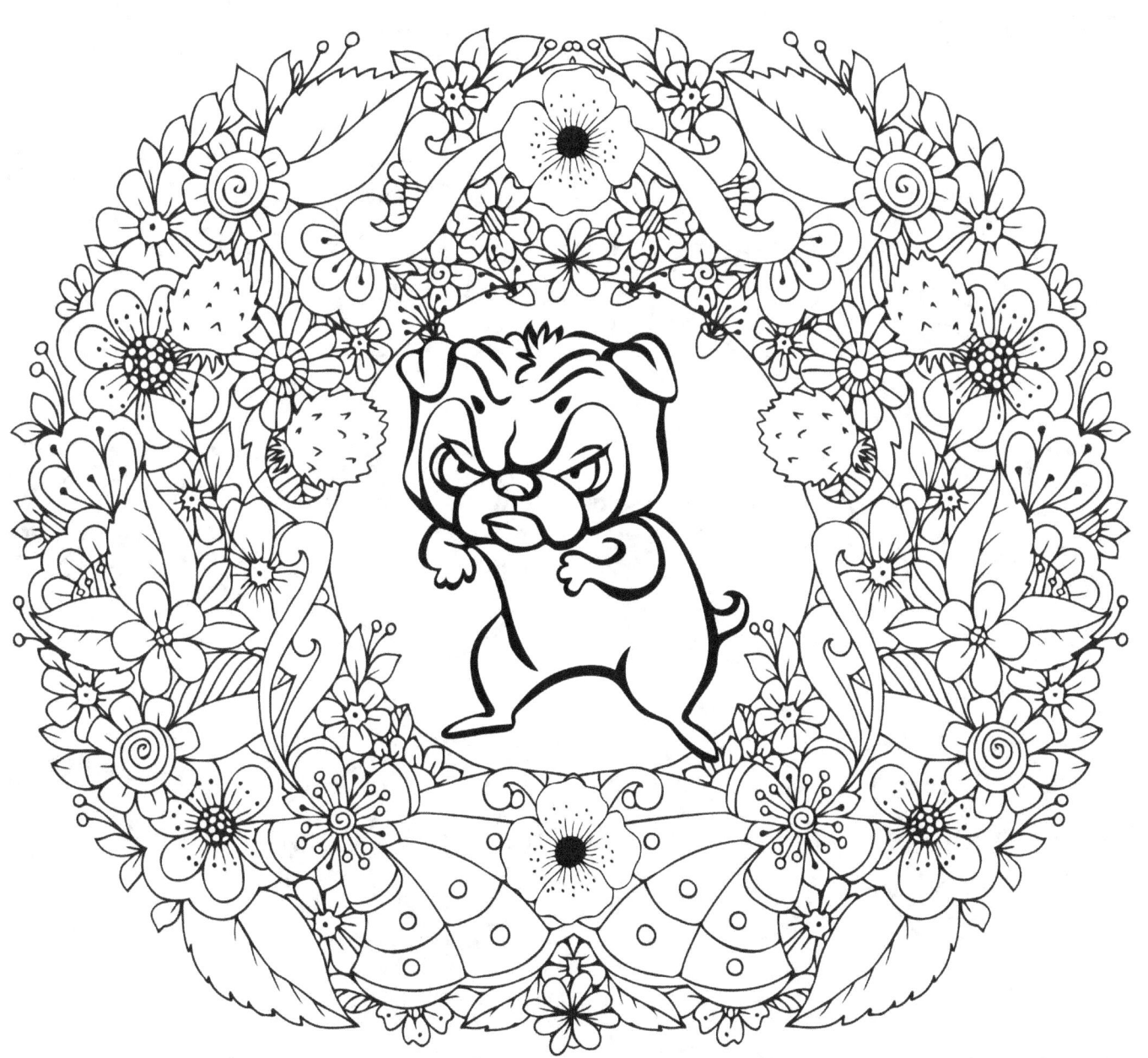

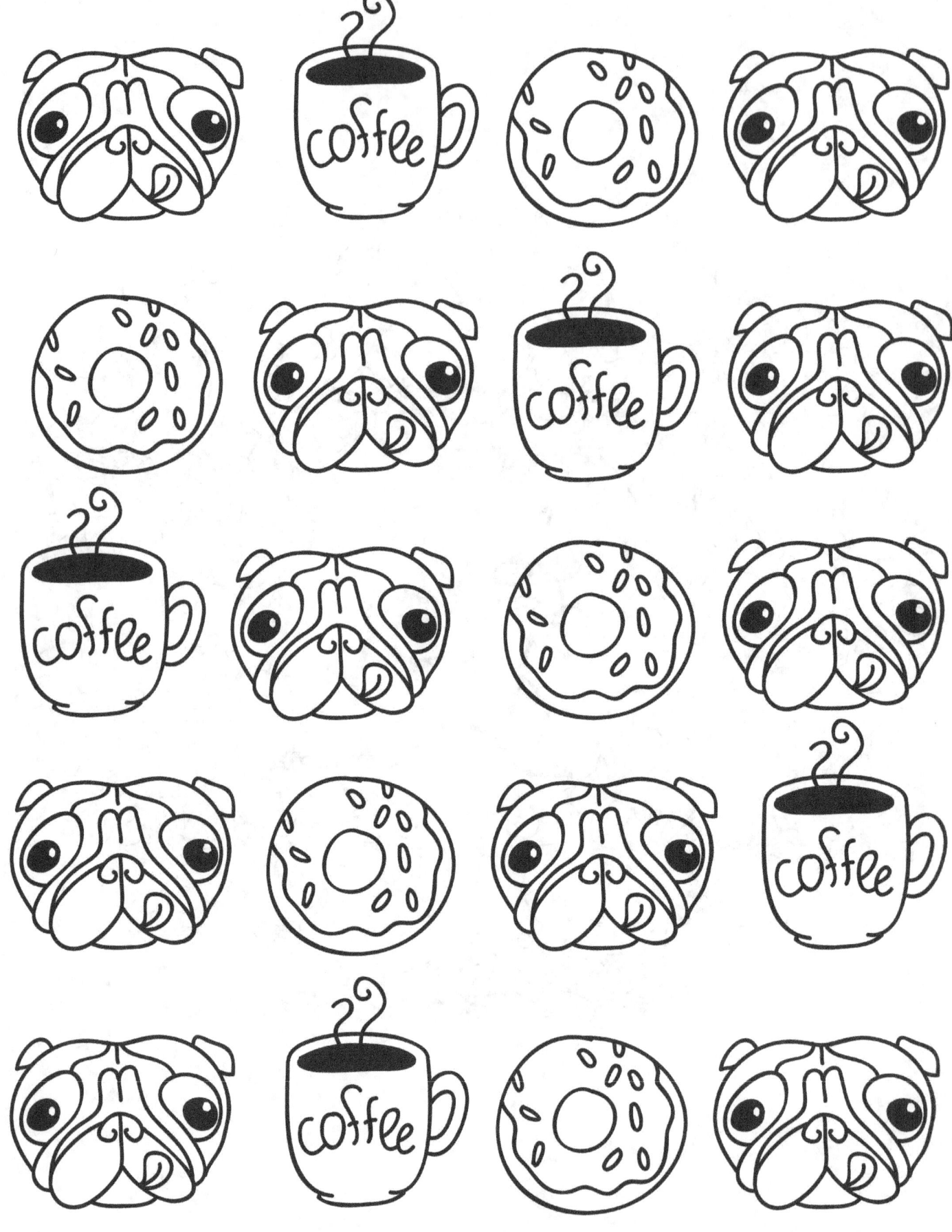

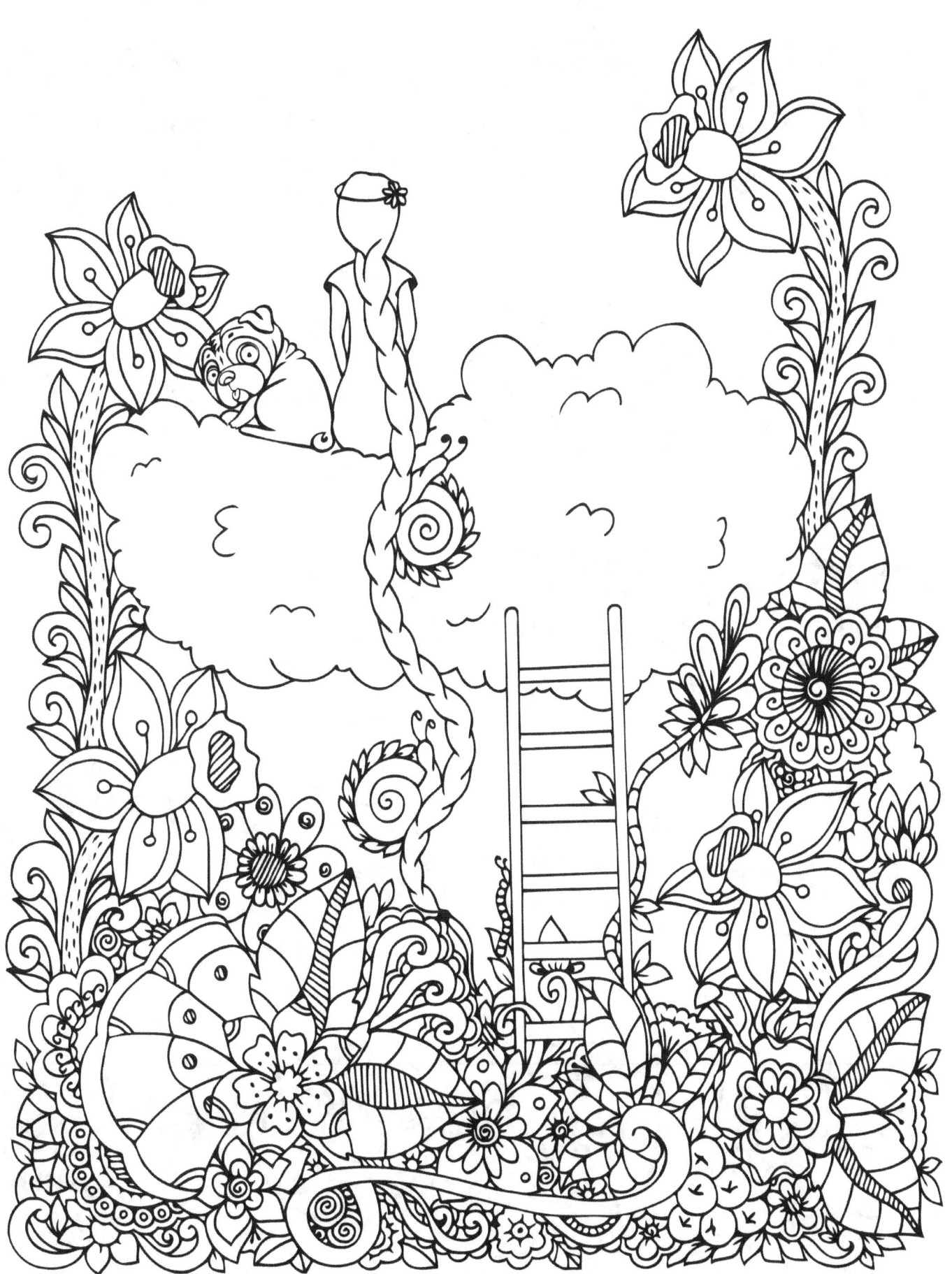

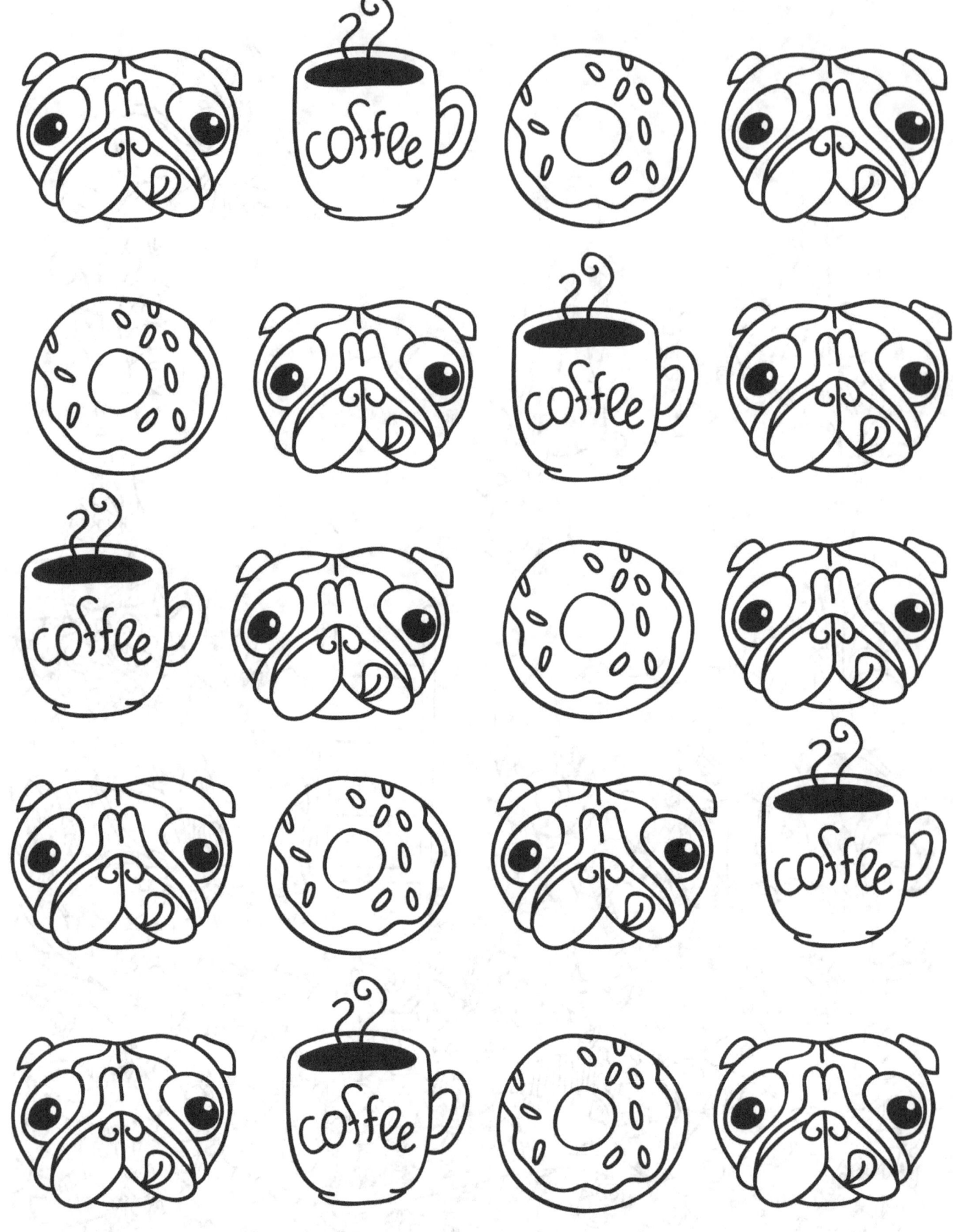

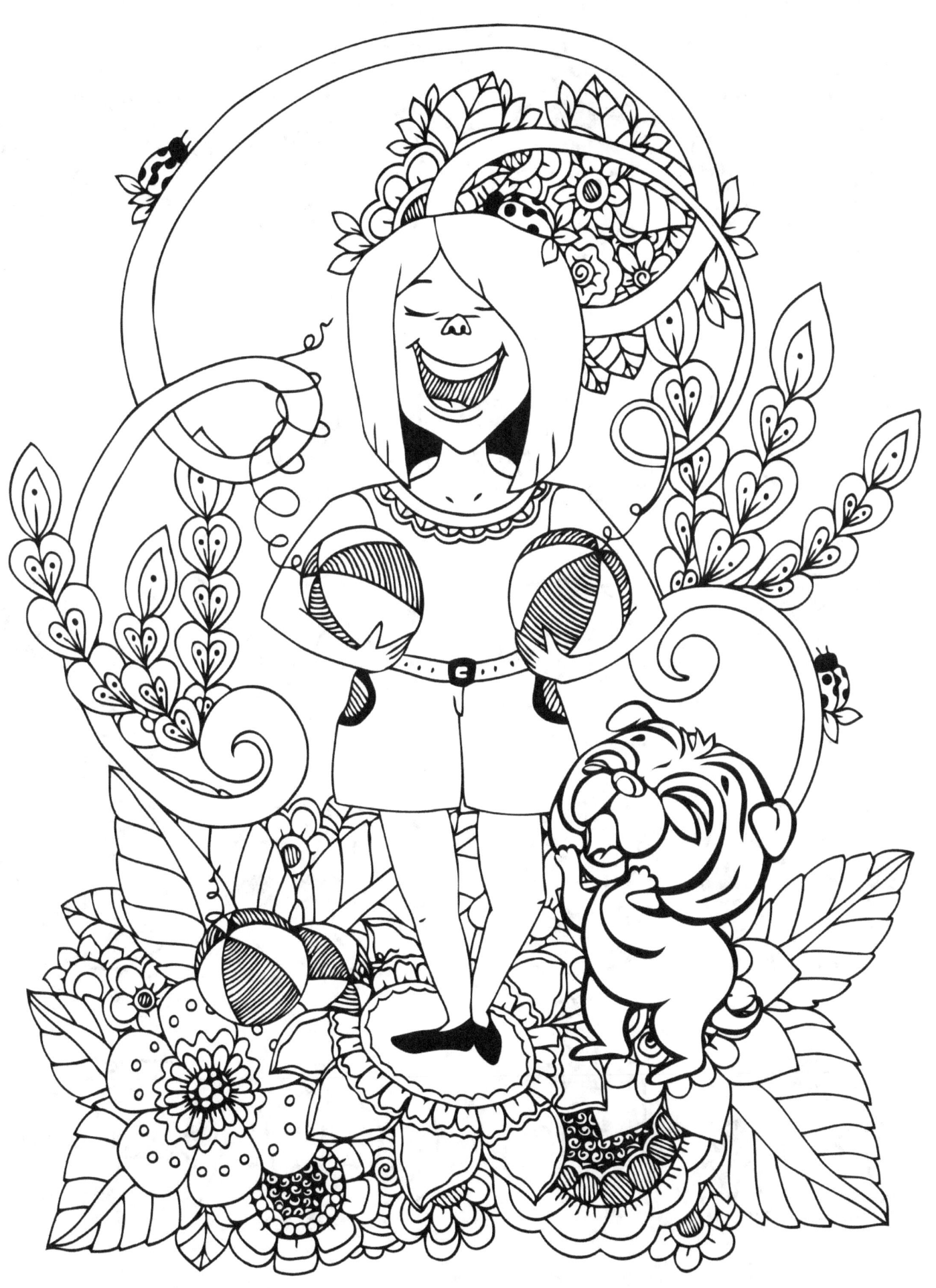

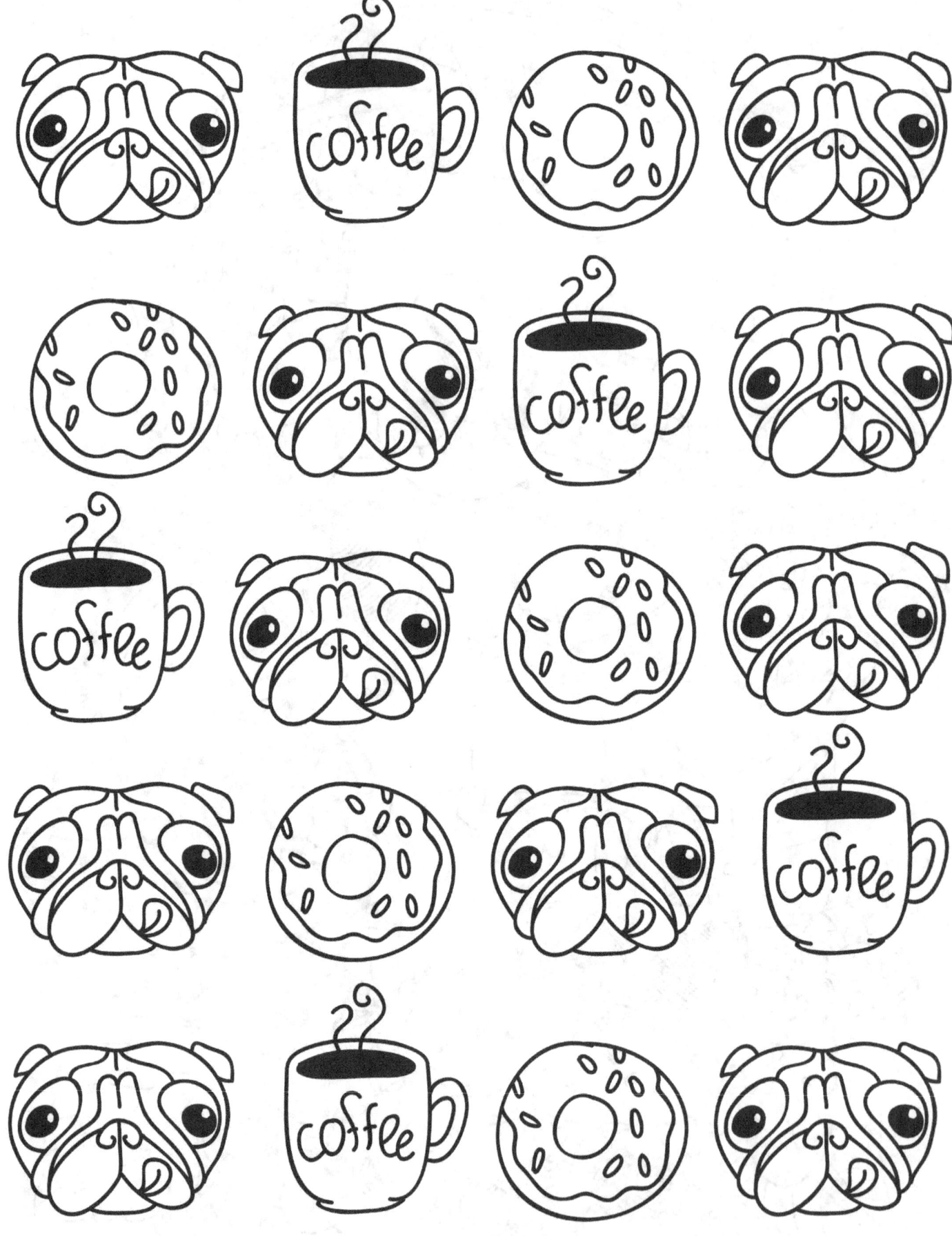

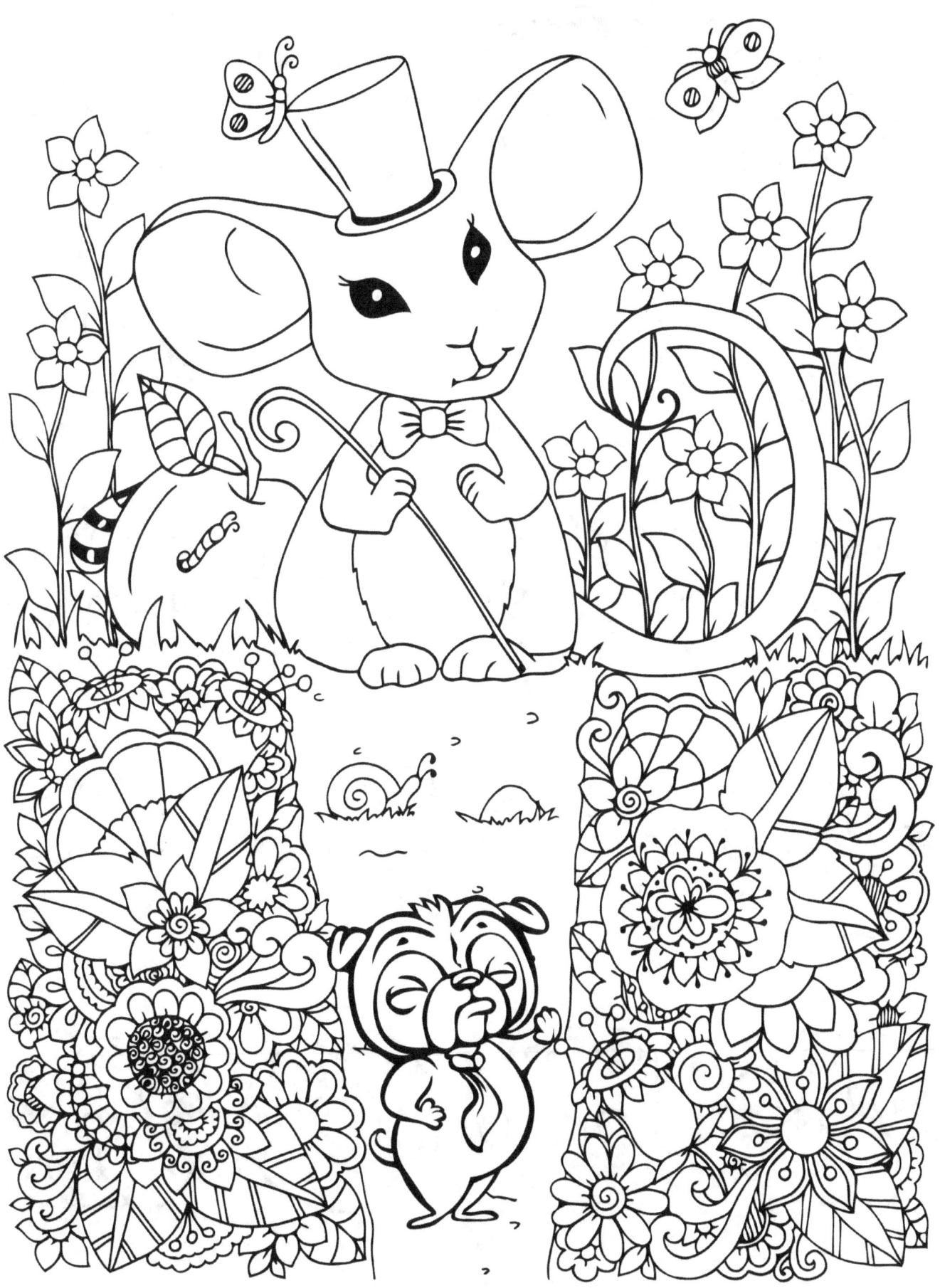

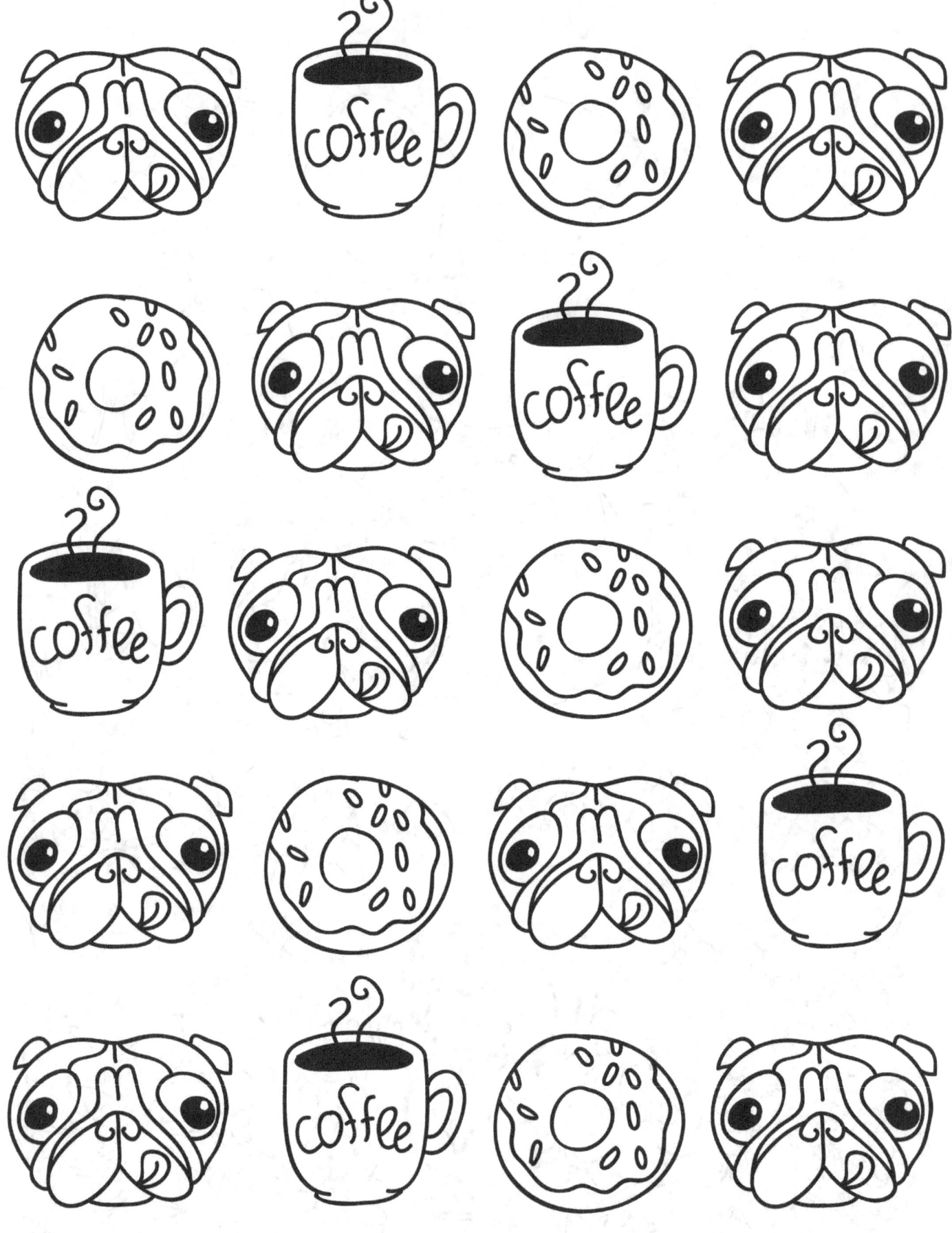

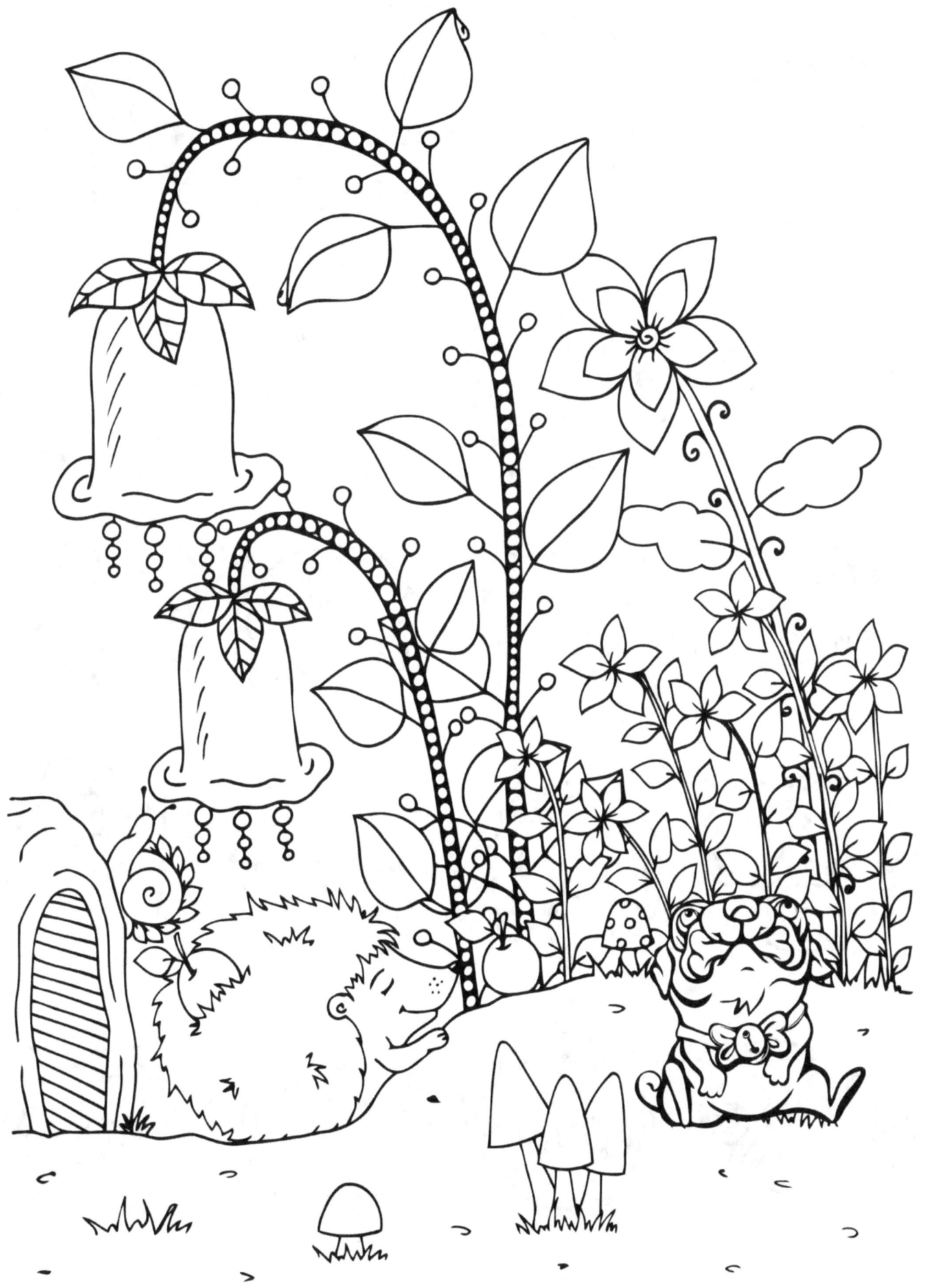

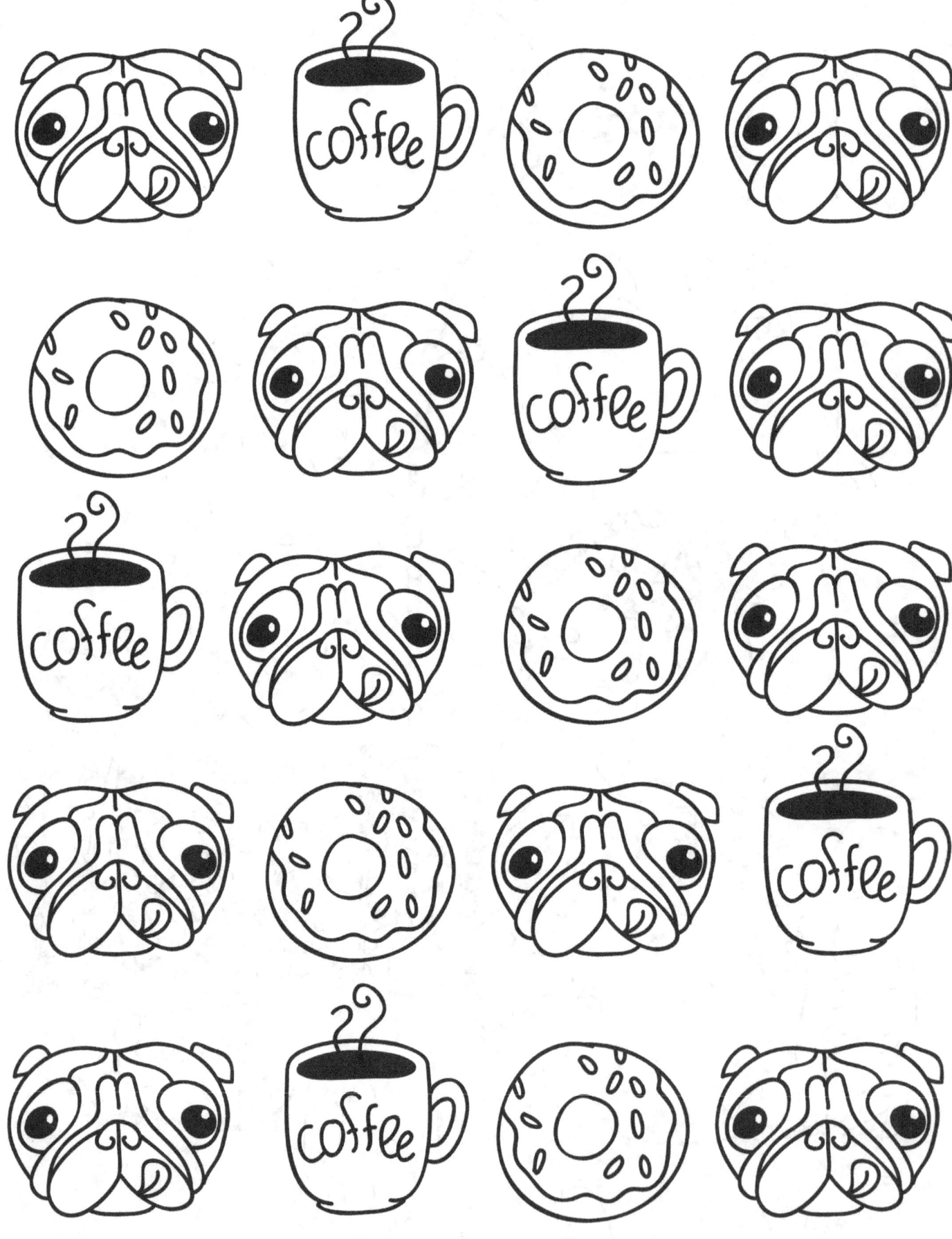

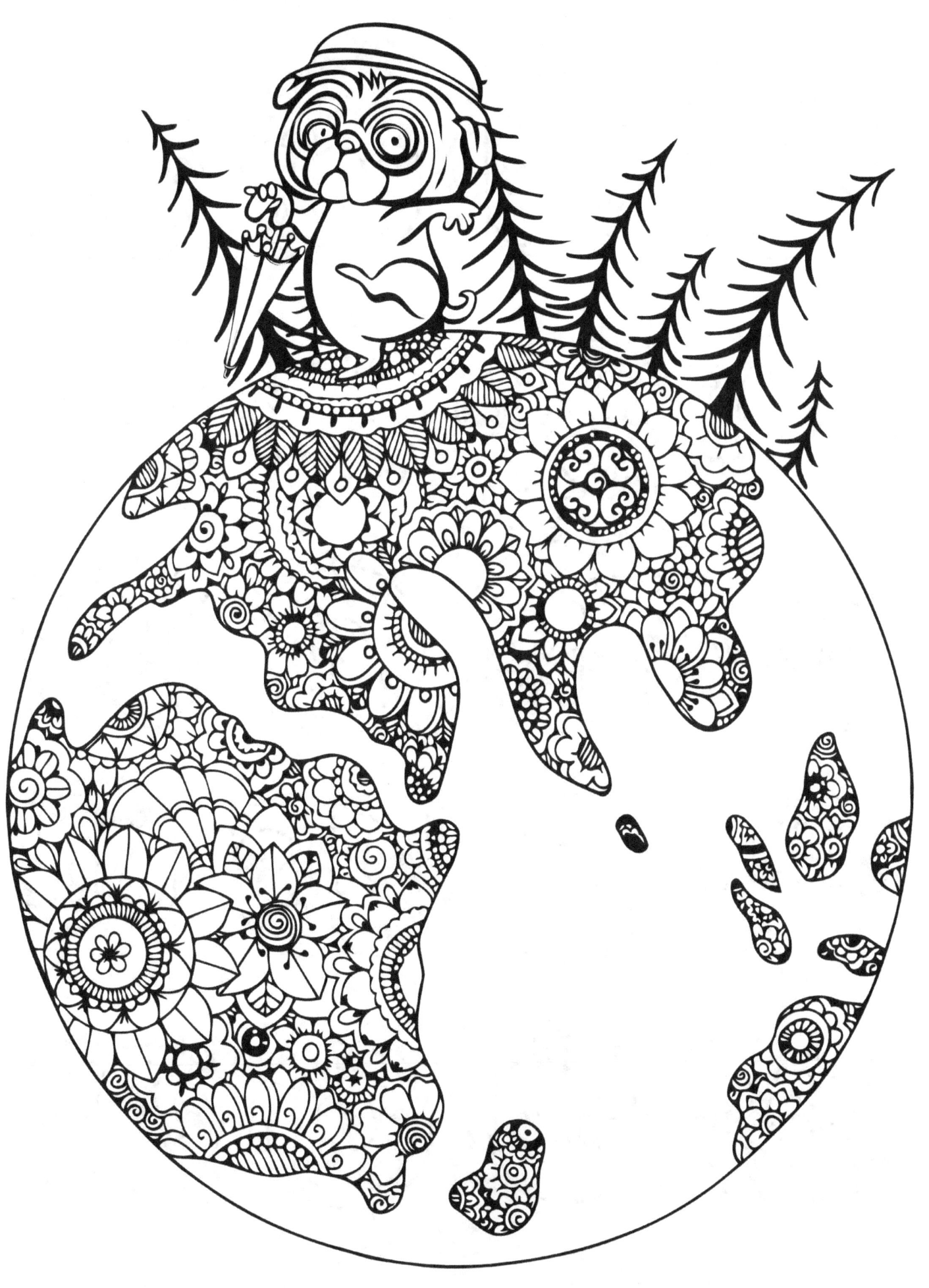

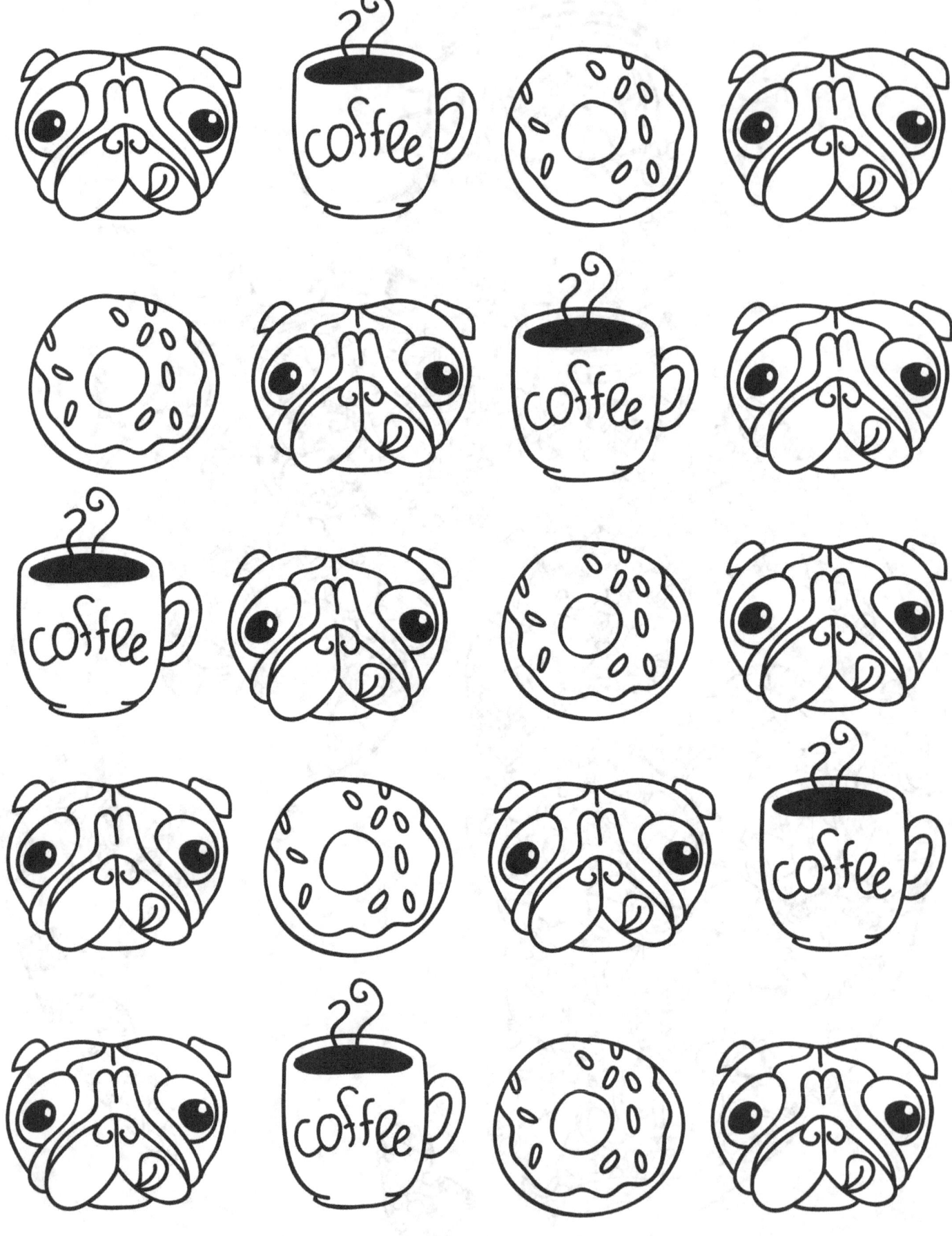

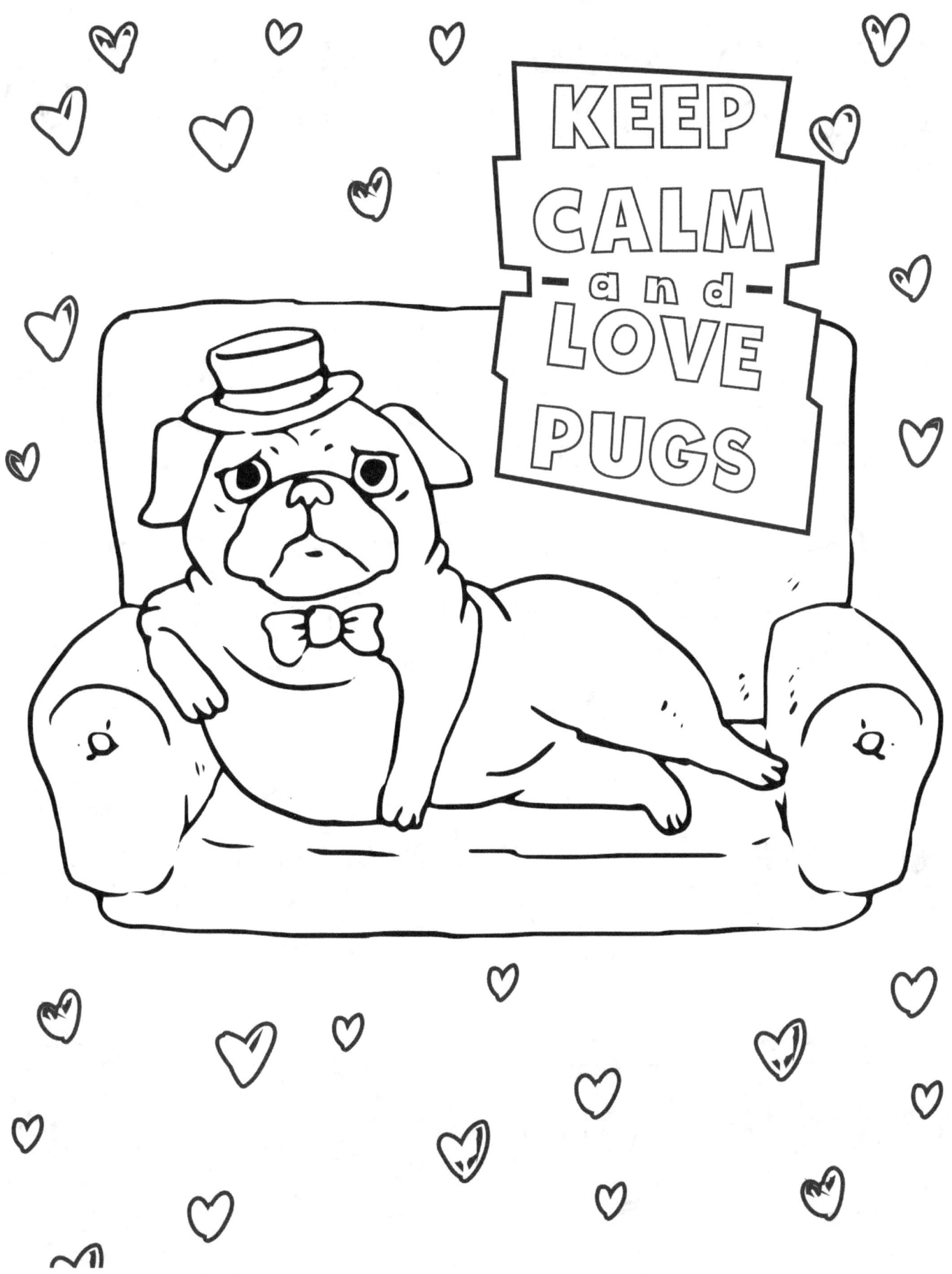

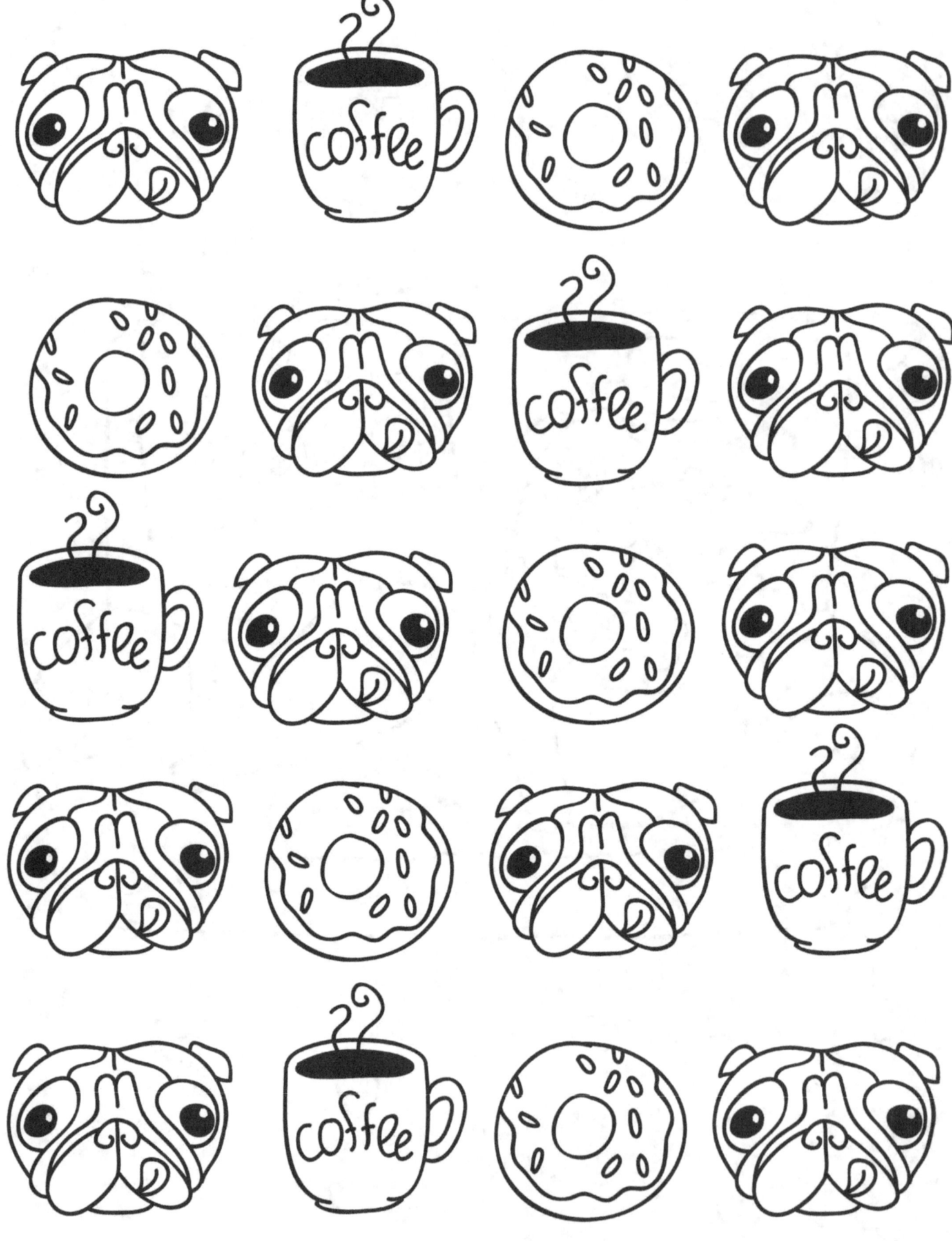

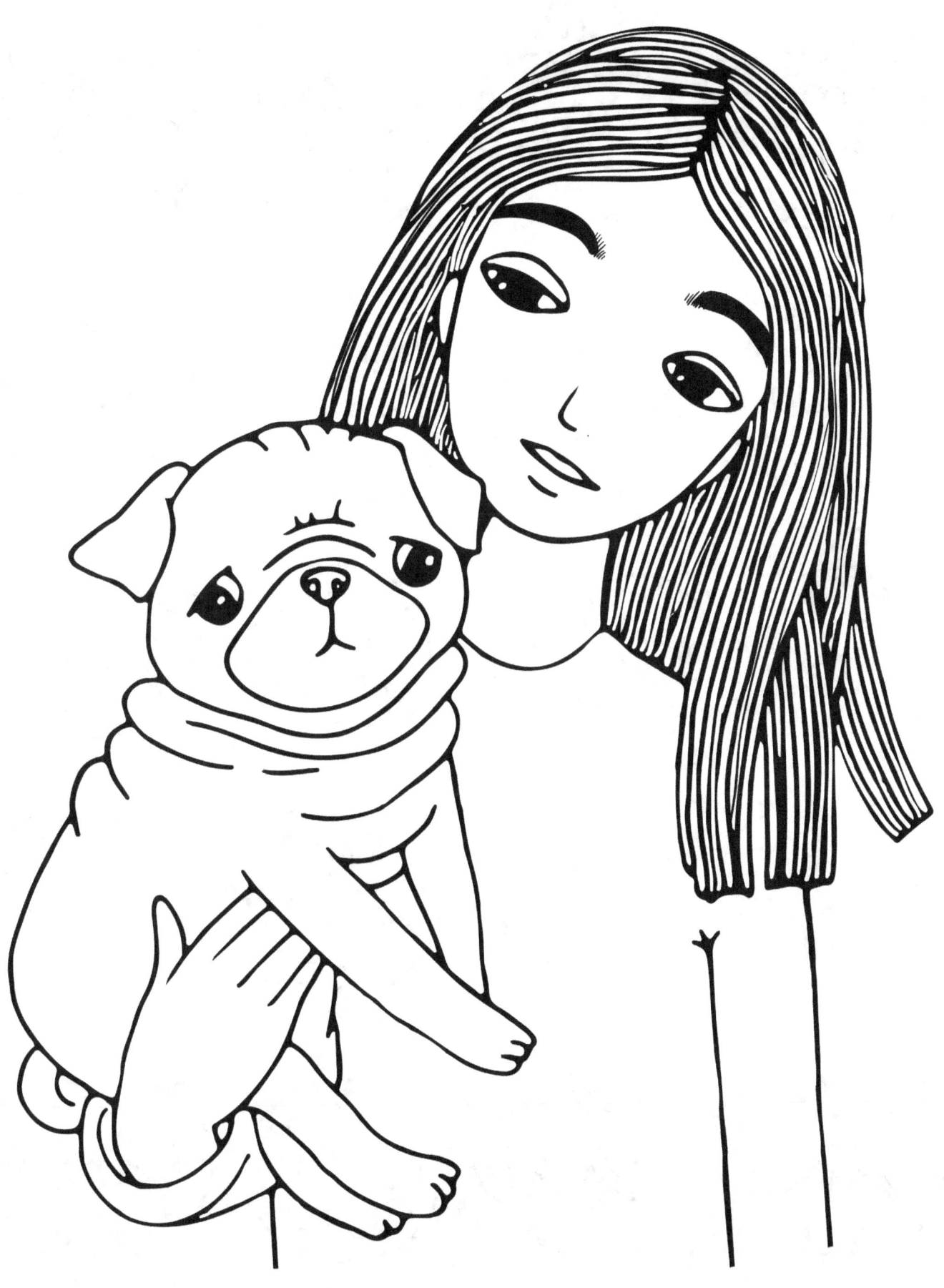

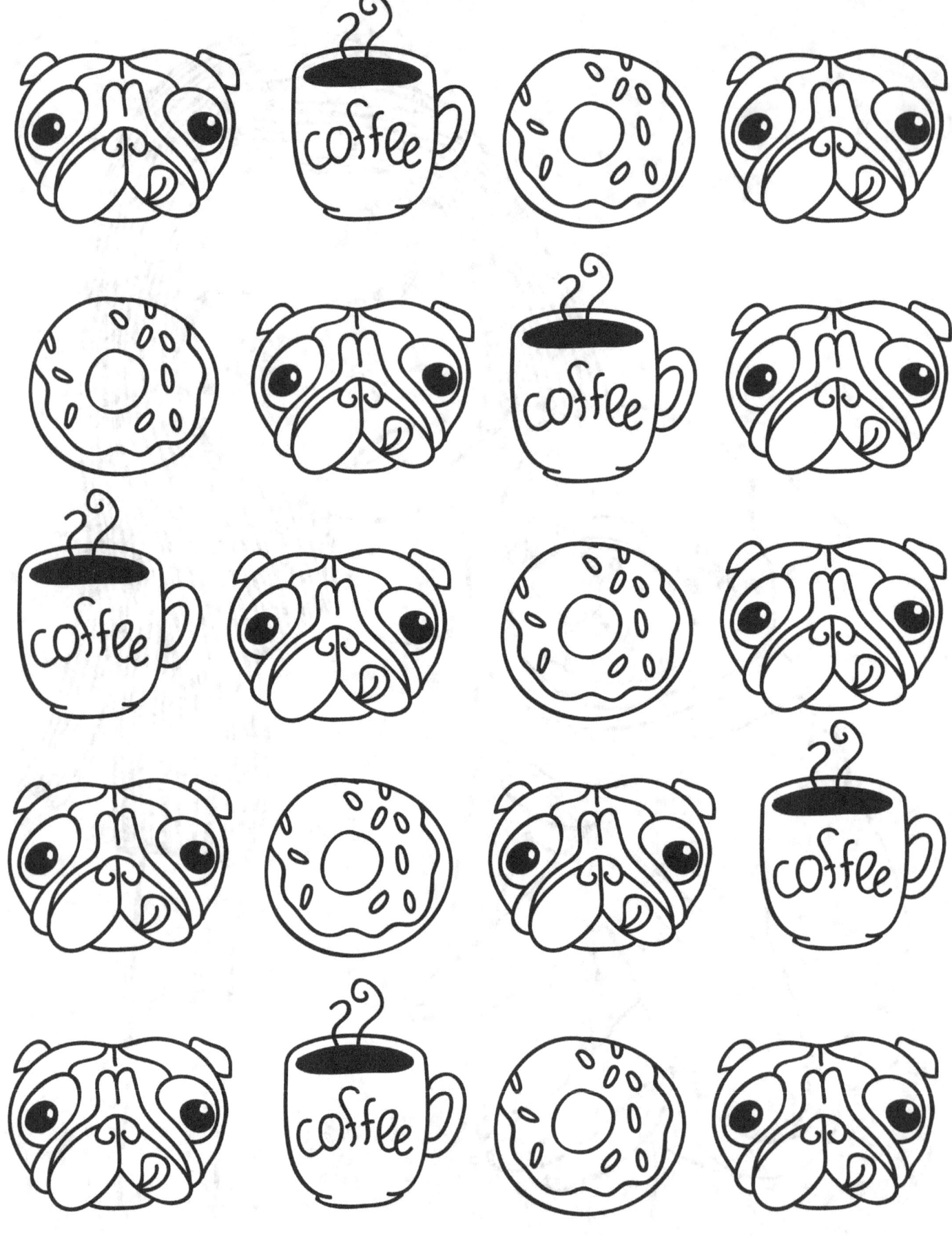

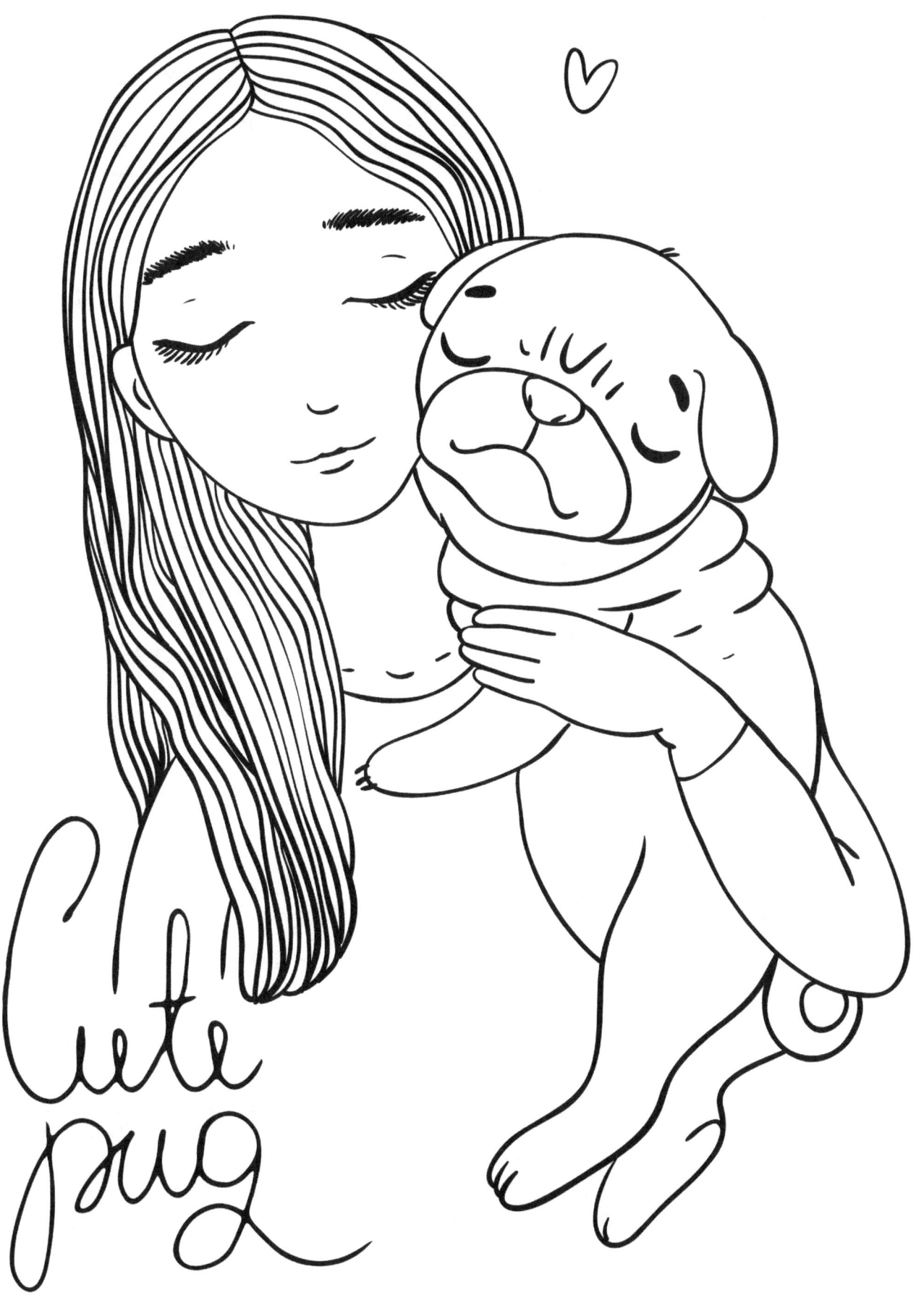

www.ingramcontent.com/pod-product-compliance
Lightning Source LLC
Chambersburg PA
CBHW080907220526
45466CB00011BA/3497